How to use Asse Learning in the ~~~~~~~~

The Complete Guide

By Mike Gershon

Series Introduction

The 'How to…' series developed out of Mike Gershon's desire to share great classroom practice with teachers around the world. He wanted to put together a collection of books which would help professionals no matter what age group or subject they were teaching.

Each volume focuses on a different element of classroom practice and each is overflowing with brilliant, practical strategies, techniques and activities – all of which are clearly explained and ready-to-use. In most cases, the ideas can be applied immediately, helping teachers not only to teach better but to save time as well.

All of the books have been designed to help teachers. Each one goes out of its way to make educators' lives easier and their lessons even more engaging, inspiring and successful then they already are.

In addition, the whole series is written from the perspective of a working teacher. It takes account of the realities of the classroom, blending theoretical insight with a relentlessly practical focus.

The 'How to…' series is great teaching made easy.

Author Introduction

Mike Gershon has been creating resources for teachers since 2009. His twenty guides to classroom practice have been viewed and downloaded over 2.7 million times by teachers in more than 180 countries.

All Mike's resources can be downloaded for free at www.tes.co.uk/mikegershon

The TES (Times Educational Supplement) website is a wonderful platform providing user-generated content for teachers, by teachers. It is an online community of professionals which reaches into the heart of classrooms across the globe, bringing great resources to teachers and learners on every continent of the planet.

Having seen how his fellow professionals responded to his resources, Mike knew he had to go that one step further and provide book-length material that could help teaching and learning in classrooms throughout the world. And so, thanks in no small part to the fantastic platform provided by the TES, the 'How to...' series was born.

For more information on Mike, his books, training and consultancy, other writing and resources, visit www.mikegershon.com

Other Works from the Same Author

Available to buy now on Amazon:

How to use Differentiation in the Classroom: The Complete Guide

How to use Assessment for Learning in the Classroom: The Complete Guide

How to use Questioning in the Classroom: The Complete Guide

How to use Discussion in the Classroom: The Complete Guide

How to Teach EAL Students in the Classroom: The Complete Guide

More Secondary Starters and Plenaries

Secondary Starters and Plenaries: History

Teach Now! History: Becoming a Great History Teacher

The Growth Mindset Pocketbook (with Professor Barry Hymer)

Also available to buy now on Amazon, the entire 'Quick 50' Series:

50 Quick and Brilliant Teaching Ideas

50 Quick and Brilliant Teaching Techniques

50 Quick and Easy Lesson Activities

50 Quick Ways to Help Your Students Secure A and B Grades at GCSE

50 Quick Ways to Help Your Students Think, Learn, and Use Their Brains Brilliantly

50 Quick Ways to Motivate and Engage Your Students

50 Quick Ways to Outstanding Teaching

50 Quick Ways to Perfect Behaviour Management

50 Quick and Brilliant Teaching Games

50 Quick and Easy Ways to Outstanding Group Work

50 Quick and Easy Ways to Prepare for Ofsted

50 Quick and Easy Ways Leaders can Prepare for Ofsted

Acknowledgements

First and foremost I must thank Jeremy Hayward, who taught me to teach. He has been a major influence and he is, without doubt, the best teacher I know. Thanks also to the many great teachers I have had over the years, specifically Judith Schofield, Richard Murgatroyd, Simon Mason, Cath Nealon, Andrew Gilliland, Graham Ferguson, and Simon Ditchfield. I must also thank all the wonderful teachers I have worked with and learnt from at Central Foundation Girls' School, Nower Hill High School, Pimlico Academy and King Edward VI School, Bury St. Edmunds. Special mention must go to the Social Sciences team at Pimlico, to Jon Mason and to James Wright. Of course, I cannot fail to thank all the fantastic students I have had the pleasure of teaching – particularly all the members of HC and HD at Pimlico. In addition, I am greatly indebted to the people I trained with at the IOE and, in particular, to Erin, Liam, Anna and Rahwa. Finally, thanks to my mum for her unfailing support over the years and her wonderful example.

I have picked up many of the activities, strategies and techniques in this book from the countless wonderful people I have worked with, however, any errors or omissions remain my own.

Table of Contents

Chapter One - Introduction

Welcome to *How to use Assessment for Learning in the Classroom*. This book will help you understand what assessment for learning is and how you can make it a part of your teaching.

This is a practical book. It will make your life easier, save you time and help your students to make great progress.

A wide range of activities, techniques and strategies are outlined in the following pages. These can be used immediately with little or no alteration. Most of what is in this book can be read and then implemented with instant effect. In addition, everything is generic and can be used across the curriculum and with different age groups.

In short, you hold in your hands the key to simple, effective and practical assessment for learning. All that is left is for you to put the ideas into practice.

What is Assessment for Learning (AFL)?

Assessment for learning is simple and effective. It involves the following three things:

1) Getting information from students about what they have learnt and using that information to inform teaching.
2) Helping students to understand what their learning is being judged against and encouraging them to think about and use assessment criteria.
3) Giving feedback which shows students what they have done well and which explains how they can improve.

The first point means that teaching is more effective, efficient and responsive. It is based around what students know and what they can do, rather than being an inflexible procession through the curriculum.

The second point means that students will come to appreciate what assessment is about, how it works and what it is for. They will develop knowledge about the assessment criteria used to mark their work. This means they will be better placed to produce work which meets the demands of the subject or topic. In addition, they will come to understand how to identify their own strengths and targets. This will help them to take control of their own learning.

The third point means that students are given formative feedback. This is feedback which is about their learning. It helps them to understand what they have done well and what they need to do to improve. By giving a comment which is made up of three strengths and a target, a teacher will assist students in making progress. This is because they will be helping them to realise what constitutes good work in the subject (through the strengths), they will be motivating them through praise (the strengths), making it clear what needs to be done to get better (the target) and how to go about this (the target).

Now, let's say that all over again, but even more simply.

Assessment for learning involves three things:

1) Eliciting and using information.
2) Opening up success criteria.
3) Giving formative feedback.

Remember that and you're halfway there!

How does the book help me to do all this?

This book contains the following chapters:

1. Introduction

The second, third and fourth chapters provide you with thirty techniques for eliciting information from your students. These are broken down into three divisions: individuals, groups and the whole-class. By using these techniques you can check the learning of your students. You can then use this information to inform your teaching and planning.

The fifth and sixth chapters provide you with a wide range of peer- and self-assessment activities. Most of these require few if any resources and can be implemented quickly and easily. By using the approaches and techniques in this chapter you will help to open up the assessment process for your students.

The seventh chapter contains two hundred example strengths and two hundred example targets. These are generic and can be used as they are, or adapted for the age-group and subject you are teaching.

The eighth chapter contains information about the general and subject-specific criteria we use to judge student work. Lists are provided which will help you to identify strengths and targets concerning the work your pupils do. By using and developing the examples in this chapter you will be able to give students quality formative feedback which helps them to make progress. You will also save time.

The ninth chapter picks out some of the factors which work against AFL, the tenth chapter show you how to overcome these, and the eleventh chapter provides a brief summary.

So, before we go on, what exactly is formative assessment?

There are two types of assessment used in schools: formative and summative.

Formative assessment = assessment *for* learning = written or oral feedback which explains why work is good and how it can be improved. For example:

This is an excellent piece of work Johnny.

Strengths:

- You have shown a clear understanding of the meaning of democracy.
- You have used examples to illustrate the different aspects of democracy.
- You have suggested aspects you think are most important. This shows you are confident in making judgements about democracy.

Target:

- Assess the advantages and disadvantages of democracy. By doing this you will demonstrate that you can think critically about the topic. You might start off by saying: 'The advantages of democracy include...'

Summative assessment = assessment *of* learning = a grade or number summing up the level of the work. For example:

Well done Johnny. 72%.

Now, clearly one of these approaches helps the student to learn and one does rather less. I will leave it to you to work out which is which.

How do I use formative and summative assessment?

As a teacher it is important to keep track of your students' progress. When you mark their work, keep a record of the summative results. Share this with your pupils at pre-determined points in the year. I would suggest three or four times is enough, although it may differ depending on the age group.

Other than that, always use formative assessment with your students. Giving them targets and showing them what they have done well will help them to learn. Giving grades, marks and levels will not. If you give the two together, the summative assessment will detract from the formative assessment. Try it and see – students will immediately start asking each other what they got and practically ignore the strengths and targets.

To make sure that the targets you set are followed-up, keep track of them. Stick a tracking sheet in the front of students' books. They can then write their targets in this as they go along. You might also leave a space where they can explain how they have met each target. Such a system will help to ensure all pupils make progress. Three ways to ensure that students make use of the targets you set them are:

- Ensure you give some lesson time over to talking about and meeting the targets.
- Refer to the targets. Encourage students to refer to them as well.
- Before pupils begin a major piece of work, ask them to write their target at the top of the page and then to write a paragraph at the end explaining whether they have achieved this or not.

How do I know that assessment for learning works?

I think it is logically deducible from the premises. Without going into an extended analysis, consider this:

- Getting information from students about their learning and using this = teaching that is more geared toward student needs.
- Students with a better idea of the criteria being used to assess their work = students who have a better idea of what they should be trying to do.
- Giving feedback which shows what students have done well and how they can improve = students who know what is good and why, and who know what improvements to make and why.

There is also a strong evidence base behind assessment for learning. The book which details the original research is:

Assessment for Learning: Putting it Into Practice, by Paul Black, Chris Harrison, Clare Lee, Bethan Marshall and Dylan Wiliam (Open University Press, 2003)

This is an excellent book. I would strongly recommend you read it. In addition, the following booklets explain the research:

- Inside the Black Box, by Paul Black and Dylan Wiliam (Letts, 1990)
- Working Inside the Black Box, by Paul Black, Chris Harrison, Clare Lee, Bethan Marshall and Dylan Wiliam (Letts, 1990)

There are a number of other booklets in the series. These focus on specific subjects and on the primary classroom. They are all very good and well worth reading. All are in print and available to purchase online. I have read them and consider this book to be informed by the principles and ideas which they put forward. Of course, all that I have written is my own and represents my own opinions and nobody else's. Any mistakes are my own as well.

Final Thoughts

I hope you find this book useful. I wrote it because it is the book I looked for, but could not find, when I started teaching. I have written it with the classroom in mind and have tried to make everything as simple, straightforward and practical as possible. This is because I know that teaching can be a demanding job and what most of us want is things which we can use, which will help and which do not eat up a lot of time.

I will leave you with some formative feedback of your own:

Strengths:

-   You have read the introduction. This means you now know what the book is about.
-   You want to know more about AFL. This is good because it shows you want to develop your practice and help your students to achieve.
-   You understand what constitutes AFL because you have assimilated the key points made so far.

Target:

-   Read the book and make use of the activities, techniques and approaches. This will lead you to embed AFL in your teaching. You and your students will benefit as a result.

Chapter Two - Eliciting Information: Individuals

In order to assess your students' learning, you must elicit information from them. There are a variety of ways to do this. Thirty methods are detailed in this chapter. They are broken down into three divisions: individuals, groups and the whole class.

Eliciting information about students' learning brings three benefits. First, it allows you to understand where your students are at. Second, it helps you to reflect on your own teaching. Third, and most importantly, it allows you to alter your teaching and planning so as to take account of your students' learning. This means that what you do in the classroom becomes more effective and more efficient; you tailor your teaching to the needs of your pupils.

Ways of Eliciting Information from Individual Students

1) Circulating and Talking

Circulating refers to the teacher walking around the room. The metaphor draws on connotations of liquids or gases moving freely and flexibly within a structure. It also suggests a route in which all areas of importance are visited (consider the body's circulatory system).

It is not always possible for a teacher to circulate. A class prone to disruption may require long periods in which the teacher is at the front on a watching brief. In such circumstances you may want to sit students who you feel will benefit from individual attention at the sides and at the front of the room. This will make it easier for you to access them while trying to keep an eye on the class as a whole.

Circulating simply requires the teacher to walk around the room and to talk to students. The conversations will elicit information the teacher can use to help pupils or to make adjustments to their teaching. Try to talk to as many students as you can. This way, you will be checking the understanding of most of your class.

Should this prove difficult, plan beforehand which students you will visit. It may be the case, for example, that some pupils need reassurance when starting a task whereas others have a tendency to get bogged down halfway through. Use such knowledge as you possess to inform your circulation strategy.

2) Circulating and Not Talking

An alternative approach is to circulate without talking to students. Instead, you will be listening, observing or reading their work. These three approaches offer different ways to elicit information from individual students. They depend on pupils doing particular tasks – you cannot read their work if they are doing a discussion activity.

You might like to plan a range of tasks in your lessons with these varying methods in mind. Alternatively, you may choose to make use of them whenever suitable opportunities arise.

When students are engaged in discussion, you can circulate and listen to what is being said. You can choose to focus on specific students, to make comparisons between students, or to get an idea of where the class is at based on what a sample of individual students are saying.

When students are working, whether it be in pairs, groups or individually, you can observe them as you circulate. You can look for specific things or ask yourself questions, for example: who looks engaged in this task? How is Student X choosing to approach this? What body language is Student X giving off?

If you set a task in which students are required to do some writing, you can read what they have done as you are circulating. You can head out into the class with a particular set of students in mind whose work you want to read, or you may have a focus such as: 'Are pupils responding to the task as I expected they would?'

In all these examples you should talk to students if the results of your listening, observing or reading suggest it would be useful. The entry is about alternatives to talking, not its negation.

3) Marking

Marking work is one of the most common ways to get information about where individual students are at and how they are accessing the learning. You can consider the short-term, medium-term and long-term situation in the following ways:

Short-term: Marking the most recent work that pupils have done allows you to analyse how they are dealing with the current topic. You might plan your marking so that it takes place after lessons or sequences of lessons with which you feel students might have difficulties.

Medium-term: Comparing students' most recent work with what they have previously done gives you a sense of how they are engaging with the topic or subject over the medium-term. You might be able to pick out trends which need to be addressed or developments which deserve praise.

Long-term: By recording marks in a mark-book and comments on a strengths and target sheet stuck in the front of students' books (or you might opt for a sheet which just covers targets), you will be able to build up a long-term view of individual student progress. One of the advantages of using a target sheet or a strengths and target sheet is that it also allows the student to keep track of their progress.

4) Reading and Not Marking

As a teacher, you can feel compelled to mark books every time you look at them outside of a lesson. This is not helpful or practical. In the first case this is because useful feedback is more likely to be provided when there is a good amount of work on which to base a judgement. In the second case this is because to mark many books very frequently can be inefficient – it is better to mark the same number of books at regular intervals and to provide richer feedback on each occasion.

If you can get past the compulsion to always mark, you will be able to pick out books belonging to certain students and read them in between lessons so as to elicit information about where they are at and how they are getting on with the learning.

A great deal can be gained from reading through a workbook which belongs to a student you are concerned about or who you feel you do not know that well. The key is to look at their book on that occasion in order to elicit information. Leave the feedback for another time.

5) Written Conversations

When you mark a student's work, you might like to include one or two questions in your formative feedback. These will help you to start a written conversation with the pupil. Questions should be related to the learning and might take one of the following forms:

- Questions of clarification.
- Questions in which the student is being asked to expand on their answers.
- Challenging questions designed to push the student's thinking.

- Questions which draw on a specific part of the learning with which you feel the student is struggling.
- Reflective questions which encourage the student to tell you about their feelings and experiences in relation to the learning.

You will need to give students time to answer your questions when you return their books.

This method can be particularly good for eliciting information from pupils who, for whatever reason, do not like to talk in class. It is also useful for communicating with students who lack the confidence to speak at length about their learning.

6) Whole-Class Feedback Techniques

You can use all of the techniques detailed in the 'Whole-Class Feedback' section to elicit information from individual students. Simply employ one of the techniques having first considered which pupils you are particularly keen to focus on. You need not convey this to those students – it may even be counter-productive to do so (for example, it might be inhibiting or it might make them feel embarrassed at being singled out). An example is as follows:

You want to find out how three students who have recently been moved into your class are accessing the current topic. Let us imagine that they have joined halfway through and that you are therefore uncertain as to whether their understanding is similar to the rest of the class or not.

You plan a review exercise in which you display a series of questions on the board with four answers, labelled A, B, C and D, for each. Students hold up cards with a letter on. This letter corresponds to what they think the answer is.

On conducting such an activity, you would pay close attention to the students in who you were interested. This would involve three things. First, observing their initial responses to the questions and answers – were they nonplussed or did they seem at ease? Second, observing what they did next – did they appear to think about the answer or did they turn to others for help? Third, observing what answers they displayed – were they correct? Were they identical to, and perhaps informed by, those people sat near to them?

7) Questioning

Questioning can be used to elicit information from individuals and from groups. Here are three methods on which you can call, depending on what type of information you would like to acquire:

Targeted questioning: Decide in advance which students you will question and what questions you will ask them. The purpose is to identify who in the class you would like to get information from and what you would like that information to be about.

Open questions: These questions invite pupils to talk at length and in depth about their thoughts and ideas. For example: What do you think about that? What might the answer be? How might you explain that? The key is to elicit information concerning reasoning; open questions allow you to analyse the thought processes which underpin what students think. Due to this fact, they are of much greater benefit than closed questions.

Questions based on Bloom's Taxonomy: Bloom's Taxonomy is a categorisation system for thinking processes. It runs as follows: knowledge; comprehension; application; analysis; synthesis; evaluation. The arrangement is hierarchical. The lower levels are simpler and more accessible than the higher levels. When asking individual students questions, use keywords connected to different levels of the taxonomy to elicit information about where students are at and how effectively they can engage with the content of the learning.

8) Discussion Tasks

Discussion can be conducted in pairs, threes, larger groups or in a whole-class setting. It can be led by the teacher, by individual students, or it can take place without someone designated as 'in charge'.

Discussion activities allow the teacher to listen to what students are saying. If you structure tasks so they include open questions, build on prior knowledge and are sufficiently scaffolded, you will find yourself in a position where most or all students in the class are able to talk in detail about the topic.

This means that information is flowing forth throughout the room. If you are leading the discussion, you might like to focus on specific students in order to find out what they think and how they are thinking. It is important to remember that the latter is as important as the former. If a student is giving correct answers but arriving at them through a misconceived method, this is likely to spell trouble later on. If you are not leading the discussion, move around the room and listen to what is being said in different pairs and groupings.

9) Random Feedback

If you ask a question, wait for pupils to put their hands up and then choose one of these students to answer, you will not elicit any information regarding most of the class' learning. There are two reasons for this. First, it is likely that in every class there will be students who are confident and/or knowledgeable. These pupils usually seek to answer most questions. If you allow them to, then you will be ensuring they share their knowledge with their peers but you will not be discovering anything about the learning and understanding of your other students. Second, speaking in public can be intimidating, particularly for children. Many may be reluctant to put their hands up for fear of embarrassment or for fear of giving the wrong answer.

An alternative method is to use a tool through which students can be chosen at random to answer questions or share their thoughts. It needs to be made clear that this is not a way of trying to catch pupils out, but is a method through which the teacher can learn more about their class in order to make their teaching more effective.

The following methods can be used, among others, to generate random feedback:

- Label each desk with a number. Draw numbers out of a hat at random or roll a combination of dice.
- Create a PowerPoint document with the names of all your students written one per slide. Play this at speed and press escape to stop the slideshow at random.
- Write your students' names on lollipop sticks. Put these in a jar and pull them out at random.
- Give students raffle tickets. Keep the stubs and put them in a hat. Draw numbers out at random; pupils with matching numbers answer the questions.
- Close your eyes and whizz your finger about in the direction of the class. Ask a student to shout 'Stop!' The pupil at whom your finger ends up pointing answers the question.

10) Modelling Activities

Here I refer to activities whereby students can model some part of their thinking so that it is made visible to the teacher. Give students in your class pots of Play-Doh or a selection of pieces of Lego® and ask them to model a concept linked to the lesson or to create a visual answer to a question.

Another option is to have a collection of scrap materials in your classroom. Students can use these to create sculptures which represent of their learning, their understanding of a concept, or which answer a particular question.

These types of activities can be used with groups and, inevitably, involve the whole-class providing the teacher with information about their learning. They are included here because they provide a good opportunity for the teacher to focus on what specific students produce using their modelling materials. In addition, the teacher can talk to and question these pupils about that which they have created.

Chapter Three - Eliciting Information: Groups

Ways of Eliciting Information from Groups:

1) Circulating

This is much the same as the explanation for circulating in the previous section. There are two supplementary points to add.

First, think carefully about which groups you want to visit and in what order. Depending on the make-up of the groups it may be wise to focus your attention more heavily on certain of them at the expense of others. In addition, you might feel that some groups will need more of your time if they are to provide you with the kind of information you want. For example, this could be because they themselves do not have a good handle on the task and so will require (perhaps extensive) support in forming and articulating their ideas.

Second, consider why it is that you are circulating. There are various reasons which might direct your movements around the classroom. These include:

- To ascertain whether all groups understand the task.
- To investigate students' opinions on the task.
- To find out how groups are planning to complete the task.
- To probe for misconceptions and errors in reasoning.
- To challenge groups by introducing new requirements or posing difficult questions.

2) Envoys

'Envoys' is an activity wherein the class is divided into groups and each group is given a set of resources or tasks related to a different aspect of the topic. After sufficient time has passed, one member of each group is elected as an envoy. They leave their seat and work their way around the rest of the groups in the class, teaching each one in turn about the aspect of the topic on which they have been working.

If you choose to use this activity, it offers a great opportunity to elicit information from each group. This can be done through listening to what the envoys are saying and how they are teaching their different aspects of the topic.

Given that each group will have worked together on their research, investigation or tasks, it is usually fair to assume that what the envoys say and how they say it is indicative of their group as a whole. Do be careful however, as this may not be the case if some students in the 'home' groups have disengaged or left others to do the work. In advance of the envoys leaving their seats, ensure that you observe whether or not all students are involved in the task.

3) Presentations

This is an age-old method with which most people are familiar. Students are split into groups and then present their work to the rest of the class. This provides an opportunity for the teacher to see and hear what students have done and what their thoughts are about the topic. Serial feedback – where each group goes up and presents in turn – can be monotonous. To avoid this you might like to have groups presenting to each other in pairs (with these been subsequently rotated); to select half the groups at random and ask these to present to the class; or to split the presentations over two lessons (and perhaps ask the two sets of pupils to do slightly different things).

There are various methods by which you might ask students to present their work. These include:

- Drama productions.
- Poster presentations (whereby groups make a large poster about the topic and supplement this with a spoken explanation).
- Speeches.
- PowerPoint presentations.
- Mini-lessons.

Be sure to set success criteria which will draw out the kind of information you want.

4) Group Notes

Appoint a note-taker in each group. Explain that their job is to take notes on everything the group discusses and does. You should make clear that these notes will be for the benefit of the group – so that they can see where they are at and how they have arrived there – and for the teacher – who will use the notes for their own purposes.

It is important to make clear in advance that the teacher will look at the notes in order to get an idea of what the group is doing. If this is not done, groups may feel compromised when their notes are collected in. To allay any concerns, stress that your purpose in looking at the notes is to gain information which you can use to tailor your teaching to the needs of the class.

You might like to provide note-takers with a pro-forma on which to make their notes. This could contain general areas of focus such as:

- Key things the group thinks.
- Points on which the group is in agreement.

- Points on which the group disagrees.

Or, it could include a series of sections closely tied to the task in hand. For example:

- What was said in the discussion?
- How did the group decide to approach the task?
- What role does each group member have and why?

5) Final Products

Group work can take many forms. Not all of these result in students creating something tangible. Discussion tasks, for example, will further understanding and develop knowledge through conversations that flit away into the ether. If you set up an activity that does have a physical end product, you can use this to elicit information about the group's learning. Here is an example to illustrate the point:

In a geography lesson, students are put into groups of three. They are given a large sheet of paper and a selection of modelling materials. The task is to create a juxtaposition of a rural and an urban environment and to label the key features of each. The extension task is to provide a written explanation of the model. The super-extension task is to identify similarities and differences between the two environments, to highlight these on the model and to supplement them with a written analysis which is cut out and stuck on.

Each group will produce a model of a rural and an urban environment. It is likely that most will also provide some written materials in supplement. The teacher will be able to examine the models and the writing in order to see how well the different groups understand the two environments. They will be able to identify any errors or misconceptions and address these in the next lesson. In addition, if most groups have reached the super-extension task, the teacher will be able to conclude that, in future, the bar can be raised.

6) Status Updates

On a certain well-known social networking website, members are encouraged to write 'status updates'. These are short sentences which indicate what that person is doing or thinking at the present time. You can make use of this idea in order to elicit information about how the groups in your class are accessing the learning.

When students have been put into groups, and before the task is to begin, announce that each group must select one person who is responsible for providing 'status updates' to the teacher. Explain that these students will be asked to come to the front every five minutes or so to give the teacher an update as to where their group is at.

You can display criteria or questions to structure the updates your students provide. For example:

- Does your group know what it is doing?
- Who is doing what in the group?
- How are you dealing with the task?
- What is the next thing you are going to do as a group?
- What end product are you working towards?

The frequency with which you call for status updates will depend on the overall time given over to the task. A balance needs to be achieved between eliciting regular information and giving groups enough time to get things done.

7) Whole-Class Feedback Techniques

The whole-class feedback techniques detailed in the next section can also be used to elicit information from groups. They will need to be adapted, but only slightly, so as to take account of the fact that groups will be answering rather than individuals. Here are some simple adaptations you might make:

- Give each group a number. Pick numbers at random from a hat. The group whose number is drawn has to answer a question or provide feedback on their work so far.
- Ask each group to choose a team name. Write these on separate slides of a PowerPoint document. Play the slideshow at speed and press escape to make it stop. The group whose name is on the main slide is the group who answers or provides feedback.
- Give each group a different coloured piece of card. This need only be a small square piece and should be looked after by a responsible member of each group. Keep your own set of similarly coloured pieces of card. Put these in a bag and draw one out at random. The group who has that colour answers the question or provides feedback.

A minor difference to whole-class feedback of which you ought to be aware is that groups will need time to confer before they give you their answers or feedback. This allows them to answer as a group, rather than as individuals. The discussion time lets them reach a consensus (or a position in which dissent is acknowledged). This means that you will be eliciting information which is indicative of the group, rather than of what one individual thinks the group believes.

8) Give Group Members Numbers

When students are in their groups, give each group member a number. These should be based on the number of people in each group. If the groups are made up of three students, number the students one, two and three. If each group contains four students, assign the numbers one, two, three and four.

Explain that, during the task, you will call out numbers at regular intervals. The students to who these refer should take a moment to discuss with their group the following three questions:

- What are we doing next?
- What have we done well so far?
- What problems have we come across?

When they have agreed answers with their group, they should come to the front and share these with the teacher. This information can then be acted on if required.

The numbers for providing feedback can be selected at random, they can be cycled through in order, or they can be chosen deliberately so the teacher gets to hear from certain students.

9) Success Criteria

This method of eliciting feedback from groups is best used when you want to reflect in between lessons on where your students are at and how they are accessing the learning. It works as follows:

Before beginning a task, provide a set of success criteria or develop a set in conjunction with your students. Explain that groups should use these to help them plan and develop their work. With around ten minutes of the lesson left, stop the class and indicate that you would like each group to produce a short written reflection detailing how close they feel they are to meeting the success criteria.

You might like to provide a pro-forma which students can fill in. A simple example would contain the following questions:

- What success criterion are you looking at?
- How have you met it?
- What could you do to improve?

These could be repeated a few times on the same sheet of paper so as to reflect the total number of success criteria there are.

Groups hand their reflections to you on their way out of the classroom. You can then examine these before the next lesson (or the next time you do group work) and use them to inform your teaching and planning.

10) Task Check-List

Create a task check-list and designate one person in each group who is responsible for filling it in. The check-list should contain a record of everything that each group will need to do in order to complete the task successfully. You might also like to include extension items and indicate that groups who complete these as well as the main set of items are likely to produce higher quality work (which will therefore achieve a higher mark).

As the lesson progresses, you can walk around the room and look at different group's checklists. This will ensure that at any one time you are in a position to know where each and every group is at in relation to the task. If a particular group is falling behind, you will be able to pick up on this immediately and give them the support they need.

At the end of the lesson you should collect the checklists in. Before you do, ask the students who are responsible for them to write the names of the pupils in their group at the top of the page. This way you will be able to reflect after the lesson on which groups have achieved what and how this might relate to their composition.

Chapter Four - Eliciting Information: The Whole Class

Ways of Eliciting Information from the Whole Class:

1) Post-It® Notes

Post-It® Notes are a great way to elicit feedback from your whole class. This is because they are sufficiently cheap and flexible for all students to be given one (or more) and for these to be annotated in a short space of time. Here are three ways you might use Post-It® Notes:

- Give each student a Post-It® note. Ask or display a question, or provide students with a statement to which they should respond. Pupils write their answers on their notes. The teacher collects these in and looks at them before the next lesson. Consider in advance whether you want students to append their name to the answer they write.

- Display a question or statement on the board. Give each student a Post-It® note. Ask them to write their response and to then stick this on the board. The teacher can look through these as students are coming up and placing them. Some can be used as the basis for discussion. Alternatively, they can be collected in by the teacher and looked at after the lesson. A final option is to invite a couple of students to spend some time sorting and analysing the different responses. They could then present their findings to the class.

- Give each student a Post-It® note. Ask or display a question, or provide students with a statement to which they should respond. Pupils write their answers on their notes. Next, they hold these up in the air so the teacher (and other students) can see them. Further questioning and discussion then ensues.

2) Mini-Whiteboards

Mini-whiteboards (which must be supplemented by dry-wipe pens and board rubbers) are a more expensive method of eliciting whole-class feedback. Their functionality is high, however, and they tend to be durable. It is likely that, should you purchase a set, they will prove good value for money in the long-term. At the time of writing, you can get a pack of thirty whiteboards and pens for approximately thirty pounds. Board rubbers could be replaced by jay cloths (cut these into smaller pieces to save money). Here are five ways you can use mini-whiteboards to elicit information from your class:

- Ask students a question and tell them to write their answers on their whiteboards. They then hold these up so the teacher and other students can see what has been written.
- Display three faces on the board. One should be happy, one in the middle, and one glum. They should be accompanied by sentences such as: 'I am confident with the learning'; 'I feel OK about the learning'; 'I do not feel confident about the learning'. Ask students to draw the face which most represents how they feel and to hold this up for all to see.
- As above except with the numbers one to five instead of smiley faces. This allows a wider range of responses.
- Ask students to write on their whiteboard what they feel has been the 'muddiest point' of the lesson. This is the thing that is least clear to them, or that is causing them the greatest difficulty. They then hold their whiteboards up in the air.
- Ask pupils to respond to a question or a statement given certain guidelines. For example: through drawing; by using

exactly seven words; through an equation. They then hold up their answers.

3) Exit Passes

An exit pass is a slip of paper which students must hand in on their way out of the classroom. They should write an answer to a question which the teacher has set, or a response to a statement or task, on their slips. The teacher will need to decide whether this is to be done anonymously or whether students should write their names along with their answers. Exit passes can be handed to the teacher, collected in by a student or placed in a box (akin to a poll booth) positioned on the teacher's desk or near the door.

Before the next lesson, the teacher can look through the exit passes and use these to inform their planning. With this in mind, it is worth considering in advance what you will ask students to write on their exit passes. It may be that you believe a certain aspect of the work is likely to have caused problems or misconceptions and that you want to check whether this is the case or not. Alternatively, it might be that you are interested in how students felt about being asked to do a certain type of task or to work in a certain way. As these two examples suggest, advance planning is likely to increase the efficacy of your use of exit passes.

4) Cards

Create a set of cards which your class can use to show you what they believe is the answer to a question or what their thoughts are regarding a statement. Here are three examples of how you might do this:

- A, B, C, D cards. Make a set of cards such that every student has one with a large 'A' on it, one with a large 'B' on it and so on. Display a series of questions on the board. Each should be accompanied by four possible answers. These should be labelled: A, B, C and D. Ask students to show you which answer they believe is correct. (A, B, C, D could be replaced by four different colours or the numbers one to four).
- True/False cards. Make a set of cards which say 'true' on one side and 'false' on the other side. Hand these out to students. Display a series of statements on the board and ask pupils whether they believe these to be true or false. Students use the cards to indicate what they think is the answer.
- Agree/Disagree cards. As above except with 'agree' and 'disagree' in place of 'true' and 'false'. Suggest that if students are not sure then they should hold their card horizontally (or not hold it up at all).

Although time consuming, it is worth laminating your cards. This will increase their life-span. You might also like to store them in bundles using rubber bands. This will help you to avoid losing any.

5) Fingers and Thumbs

You can elicit information from students by asking them to use their hands. Here are three possible methods:

- Ask pupils to tell you how they are feeling about the learning by using their thumbs. Explain that they should give a 'thumbs up' if they are feeling confident, a 'thumbs in the middle' if they are feeling OK, and a 'thumbs down' if they are not feeling confident.
- Ask students to tell you how they are feeling about the learning by using their fingers. Display a set of five

statements on the board ranging from 'I feel really confident with the learning' to 'I do not feel at all confident with the learning'. These should be accompanied by the numbers one to five. Students consider which statement they most agree with and then hold up the number of fingers which correlate to it.

- Display a question on the board accompanied by three, four or five possible answers. Ask pupils to consider which one they think is correct. They should then hold up the same number of fingers as the number of the answer they believe to be right.

6) Traffic Lights

The traffic light colour scheme – red, amber, green – can be used to elicit information from a whole class. Here are three ways you might put it into action:

- Create a class set of red, amber and green cards. Hand these out to students. Ask them to display the card which tallies with how they are feeling about the learning. Green = feeling confident; amber = feeling OK; red = not feeling confident. You might ask students to show you a colour at specific times in the lesson, or you might ask them to keep a colour displayed on their desks at all times (and to change this through the lesson, as and when it is appropriate).
- At the end of the lesson, ask students to write in their books the colour which represents how they feel about the learning. If you have sufficient coloured pens available, hand these out and ask pupils to write in the appropriate colour or to draw a circle and to colour it in using the appropriate colour.
- At the end of the lesson, display the learning objective. Ask students to indicate whether they feel they have met this

or not. They should either display a colour card or make a note in their books of the colour which represents where they feel they are at.

7) Continuum

Display a statement on the board. This could take one of the following forms:

- A statement about the learning. For example: 'I feel I have understood everything we have done today.'
- A statement about the content of the learning. For example: 'Democracy is a system of government.'
- A statement which is an opinion about some aspect of the learning. For example: 'Democracy is the perfect form of government.'

Explain that one side of the room equates to 'I completely agree' and that the other side of the room equates to 'I completely disagree'. The area in between is a continuum. The central point represents 'I don't know', 'I do not feel strongly either way' or 'I am not sure'.

Invite students to leave their seats and to position themselves at the point on the continuum which correlates with their feelings about the statement. You might like to lay a piece of rope along the floor or to display a double-ended arrow on the board so as to provide a visual reinforcement of the concept of a continuum.

This activity will allow you to see what all your students think about the statement in question. You can develop a discussion based around the reasons pupils have for the positions they have chosen.

This activity involves students standing up and moving around. As such, it may not be appropriate for all classes. You will need to decide in advance whether your pupils will be able to deal with it in a sensible manner. One way of introducing it gradually, and so familiarising pupils with how you expect them to behave, is as follows:

Display the statement on the board. Ask students to draw a continuum in their books and to place themselves on this. Invite a group of students (perhaps a third of the class) to come up to the front and to place themselves on the imaginary continuum between the classroom walls. Question the students and encourage pupils who are sat down to ask questions as well. Having run the activity a few times in this way, you will be better placed to allow all students to stand up and to come to the front. Even so, it is still advisable to invite them up in tranches rather than all at once.

8) Different Answers

This activity again involves movement. It uses more of the space in the classroom than 'Continuum'. Students are given discrete rather continuous response-options. As such, the method elicits slightly different information. It works as follows:

Display a question on the board. Indicate four areas of the room and state a possible answer tied to each of these. You can do this through one of the following methods:

- Before the lesson, print off four answers to three different questions. Label the sets of answers: 'Q1', 'Q2' and 'Q3'. Divide the answers into four piles. Each pile should have a Q1 answer, a Q2 answer and a Q3 answer. Stick these on the wall at four different points in the room.
- Make four large labels containing the letters: 'A', 'B', 'C' and 'D'. Stick these to the wall at four different points in

your room. When you display a question, also display four answers which are labelled: A, B, C and D.

- Take photographs of four different parts of your room. When you display a question, also display four answers. Insert the photographs next to the answers.

Students are then invited to go to the area of the room which they believe indicates the correct answer. This allows the teacher to see quickly what all students think about a particular question.

9) Technology

There are always three questions I ask myself when it comes to using technology in the classroom:

- Is it cheap?
- Is it easy to use?
- Does it aid learning?

The following methods for eliciting information from your whole class answer 'yes' to at least two of these questions.

Voting Pods: These are small, hand-held devices which send signals to your computer. They come with software which, when installed, makes the information from the voting pods intelligible. Each pod has a number of buttons on it. These are coloured or numbered. The teacher displays a series of questions or statements on the board and students press the button on their pod which accords with what they think is the correct answer. The teacher can then display the results for the class to see, or they can analyse them in private.

Online Forums: If you have an online learning platform internal to your school, you can set up a forum to which students can contribute. You might start it off with a question, a statement or a link to some stimulus material such as a newspaper article. You can then ask students to make a comment on the forum either during the course of a lesson, or for homework. The forum will record which pupils have made comments. You will be able to use this information to inform your teaching and planning.

10) Silent Debate

This discussion activity produces a large amount of writing conveying the ideas and opinions of the whole group. It works as follows:

Write a series of statements or questions related to the topic in the middle of four or five large pieces of sugar paper. Distribute these through the classroom. Invite students to walk round in silence and to write comments on the pieces of paper. When they have done this, ask them to go round again and to comment on what other people have written. Anyone who talks is sent to the 'naughty corner' for thirty seconds.

At the end of the activity there will be a series of sheets of paper containing a wealth of information about what your students think and why they think it.

If you would like to track who writes what, divide the class into groups and give each group different coloured pens to use. While you will not necessarily be able to identify comments as belonging to a specific student, you will at least have a general idea of who came up with what (and may be able to make inferences based on a combination of the colour and your previous knowledge).

You can ask students to sign their comments. This has the potential to be quite inhibiting however and may, as a result, prove counter-productive.

Chapter Five - Peer-Assessment

Peer-assessment opens up the assessment process for students. It gives them an opportunity to use success criteria in order to make judgements. In addition, it encourages pupils to identify strengths and set targets which make use of those criteria. It thus helps students to better understand what their own work is being judged against, what good work ought to include, and how one can go about making work better.

The final point to note is that peer-assessment allows students to experience other people's work. It therefore helps them to develop a broader view of how questions can be answered, how tasks can be completed and what methods their peers are employing.

In this chapter there are twenty different entries. Each one explains an approach to peer-assessment, one or more activities you might use to structure peer-assessment, or some part of peer-assessment which is worthy of close attention.

Everything has a practical focus and can be used in any subject with any age-group.

1) Pairs

Here are three ways to do peer-assessment when students are working in pairs:

First Method: Allow between ten and fifteen minutes. This should be after a few lesson's worth of work has been completed by your students. Explain that pupils will be working in pairs to mark each other's books.

Spend five minutes revisiting what it is that you have been studying. You might want to make a list of recent lesson topics on the board, or create a spider diagram of relevant keywords and concepts. This will act as a primer for your students, making it easier for them to mark their partner's work effectively.

Students now mark each other's books. Indicate that they should identify any errors or misconceptions they come across and that they should write notes of praise for things their partner has done well. Ask them to conclude the marking with an overall comment. This should include three good things about their partner's work and one area for improvement. Finally, ask students to swap their books back. They should read through their partner's marking and then discuss it with them.

Second Method: For this activity, students should have completed an extended piece of writing. In pairs, pupils take it in turns to read their work out to each other. This should be done twice. The first time, the student who is listening ought to remain silent. The second time, the student who is listening should ask questions. They should feel free to interrupt the speaker, though their questions must be concerned with the work which is being read out. Examples of what they might ask include: questions of clarification, questions concerning structure and questions directly challenging what has been said.

At the end of the second reading the student who has been listening takes a minute or two to formulate their thoughts. They can then deliver either an oral or a written peer-assessment in which they identify a range of good things and one area for improvement. Students then swap over and repeat the process.

The teacher might ask the peer-assessors to focus on something specific. Alternatively, the pupils who are speaking may ask their partner to pay attention to something on which they would like to receive feedback.

Third Method: Students are put into pairs. The teacher sets up an activity in which each pair must work together to create something. This might be a drama performance, a joint piece of writing or an analysis of some material. When sufficient time has elapsed, the teacher asks students to get into groups of four, each containing two pairs.

In each group of four, the pairs take it in turns to share whatever it is they have produced. At the end of the sharing, the pairs then take it in turns to peer-asses each other's work.

The teacher might provide some criteria against which the assessment can take place, or groups might agree among themselves how they want to go about their assessments. This second option could include each pair stating specifically what it is they would like the other pair to focus on.

2) Threes

Here are three ways to do peer-assessment with students working in groups of three:

First Method: Two students engage in a discussion while the third student listens and observes. At the end of the discussion (signalled by the teacher calling 'time') the first two students turn to the third student. They then provide a peer-assessment concerning what they have heard and what they have seen.

It is advisable to give the third student a pro-forma or a list of criteria which they can use to order their listening and observation. This could be in the form of questions (What are they talking about? How well are they listening to one another?), or categories (Content; Listening; Responding). By doing this, you will help to ensure that there is a strong structure to the peer-assessment. If you want to give your pupils a little more scope, provide them with a range of questions or categories and ask them to choose the ones on which they will focus.

The peer-assessment itself should combine an identification of strengths with an explanation of one area which can be improved (and, if possible, a demonstration of what this would entail). The two students can then restart their discussion and attempt to put the advice into action.

Second Method: After students have produced an extended piece of individual work, ask them to get into groups of three. They should pass their work to the person on their left, who will then go through it and create a peer-assessment. Of course, if the work created is not physical – such as a piece of drama or a monologue – then the author will need to perform it or demonstrate it to the person on their left.

When the peer-assessments have been completed, one student begins the feedback process by explaining the judgements they have reached. The person whose work was assessed listens carefully. The third student listens and then, when the first student has finished speaking, asks their colleague how they feel about what they have heard. If necessary, they then ask follow-up questions to both of their fellow group members so as to facilitate a discussion of the peer-assessment. Students then swap roles and repeat the process a further two times.

Third Method: Pupils work in groups of three to create a piece of work. This can be a whole range of things, though it is advisable that it has some depth to it (otherwise, there will be little to assess).

Students clear a space on their table in which to display their work. If appropriate, ask each group to write a short summary of what they have produced or an explanation of the rationale behind it. This can be left on the table, beside the work itself.

Each group member is given a role. These are as follows: Strength-Spotter; Improvement-Identifier; Target-Setter. Groups are invited to walk around the room and to find one piece of work to peer-assess. When they have made their selection (and every piece of work must have one group peer-assessing it) the group members write out a peer-assessment. Each student contributes the section which is relevant to their role – the identification of strengths, possible improvements or a target.

Finally, groups return to their own work and read through the peer-assessment they have been given. (You might like to develop the activity by asking groups to go to more than one piece of work. Students will then end up with multiple assessments to consider).

3) Groups

Here are three ways to do peer-assessment with students working in groups (which I take to be four or five students in number):

First Method: Set a task for students to complete in groups. Plan in advance how much time you will give to the activity. When pupils have reached the half-way point, ask them to stop whatever it is they are doing.

Each group should now select two members to take on specific roles. One of these will provide a peer-assessment of the group's work so far (Student A) while another will do the same except for a different group (Student B).

The teacher should provide a set of criteria or a list of categories, related to the task, which pupils can use to make their assessments. Student A begins. They look back over the work their group has done and identify what is going well and what could be improved. After this, Student B leaves and provides the same service for another group. The key point here is that each group will get an internal and an external perspective on their work thus far.

With the peer-assessments complete, all students return to their original groups. The teacher announces that the original activity will recommence and invites groups to act on the feedback they have received.

Second Method: Set a task for students to complete in groups. This should be something which can be left out on display, for example: a poster, a PowerPoint presentation (which could be printed off or displayed on a laptop) or a collection of items based around the same topic.

Assign the following roles to your groups: Strength-Spotters; Improvement-Identifiers; Target-Setters. As has been noted elsewhere, it is always preferable to have a high ratio of positive comments to developmental comments. As such, assign three or four groups to be 'Strength-Spotters' (this is working under the assumption that you have five or six groups. Therefore, there will be three or four sets of 'Strength-Spotters, one set of 'Improvement-Identifiers' and one set of 'Target-Setters).

Invite groups to walk around the room and to assess every piece of work on display, including their own. The result of this will be that, upon returning to their work, each group will find three or four strengths, one potential improvement and one future target.

If you have fewer groups than I have outlined here, I would recommend dispensing with the 'Improvement-Identifiers'. It is more important to have a high number of positive comments than to have comments of all three types.

Third Method: Set a task for students to complete in groups. Upon completion of the activity, ask groups to pair up (it is advisable to plan ahead here and to ensure that you have an even number of groups).

In the pairings, each group should take it in turns to perform or display their work. In addition, they should talk through what it means, how it was made and the decisions which led to its creation.

Following this, the other group should provide a peer-assessment. This can be unstructured, with students making comments as they wish, or it can be structured through the use of roles as outlined above (three Strength-Spotters, one or zero 'Improvement-Identifiers' and one 'Target-Setter').

4) Hand In, Shuffle and Redistribute

This activity can be used with a single piece of work which students have produced or with their books, as long as these contain sufficient material to make the task worthwhile. It works as follows:

Collect in your class's work or their books. Shuffle these and then redistribute them. Ask students to peer-assess whoever's work or book they have been given. The teacher should provide some criteria against which assessments can be made. It may be appropriate to precede the activity with a discussion of what makes a good piece of work in this particular instance, or a reminder of what has been studied over the past few lessons.

Students should identify three good things about the work they are assessing and one way in which it might be improved. They should also offer a demonstration of how the improvement could be achieved. This latter point is important. It means that when the student has their work returned to them, they will be able to see quite clearly what it is they need to do in order to make it better. The demonstration will add value to the improvement. It will make it more accessible to the student whose work it concerns.

When peer-assessments have been completed, ask pupils to stand up and to return the work they have been marking to its author. If you do not feel comfortable with your class standing up and milling around, either collect the work in yourself and hand it out, or ask small groups of students to stand up at a time.

Ask pupils to read through the comments their peers have written. When they have done this, ask them to put the improvement which has been identified into practice. This might involve them rewriting a section of their work underneath the peer-assessment. Alternatively, it might entail them creating something new, but still related to the topic, which encompasses the improvement.

When pupils have done this, they should seek out the peer who assessed their original piece of work. On finding them, they should discuss the initial peer-assessment. Then, the two students should reflect on whether or not the subsequent piece of work has successfully incorporated the improvements which were suggested. If the answer to this is no, it will be incumbent on the peer-assessor to demonstrate why this is not the case and how the situation might be rectified.

You will note that there are three parts to this activity: the peer-assessment; the improvement of the original work; and the subsequent discussion. You do not have to do all of these in the same lesson. For example, you might like to do the peer-assessment as a plenary and combine the improvement and discussion into the following lesson's starter activity. Another option is to do the peer-assessment as a plenary and to ask for a general target rather than an improvement. In the subsequent lesson, pupils should aim to meet their target. A discussion can then take place at the end of that lesson in which the student and their peer-assessor consider whether the target was met.

5) Hand-In Anonymously, Shuffle and Redistribute

The structure for this activity is the same as that explained in the previous entry. The difference is that the work which students hand-in is anonymous. Here are three ways to ensure this:

- Students complete their work on sheets of paper but do not write their names.
- Students complete their work in their books. These are handed-in open on the page at which the work to be marked begins. The teacher hands them out and asks students not to look at the front of the books.
- Students complete their work in their books. They are then asked to stand up and to move around the room with their books. When the teacher signals, they must place their book on one of the tables in the room (not their own), open at the appropriate page. Students then return to their seats and mark the work in front of them, without looking at the front of the book.

It is likely, of course, that some pupils will recognise the handwriting of a friend. It would be a surprise, however, if a majority of students were to recognise the work that you asked them to peer-assess.

The purpose of this activity is threefold:

First, it encourages students to be objective. When receiving a piece of anonymous work, students are faced with the prospect of assessing that work solely on its merits, without being influenced by knowledge of the author (I am not suggesting that they always will be – just that by running the activity in this manner one will remove the possibility).

Second, students will often have their work peer-assessed by people who sit near them in class. This is because it is simple and straightforward for all involved. By running the activity in one of the ways indicated above, the teacher will ensure that students receive a different perspective on their work. This will be of benefit, causing them to think about what they have produced from a different angle.

Third, redistributing work which is anonymous helps to normalise the peer-assessment process. It encourages students to see the activity as one in which they are providing a service which, while personal to the work, is impersonal as regards the author. This is akin to what teachers and examiners do. It is therefore good for students because it helps them to understand the experience of those people who will ultimately mark their work.

You will need to decide how authors will get their peer-assessed work back. You may want students to find out who marked their work and to encourage discussion about the assessment. The advantage is that more might be learnt from the ensuing conversations. On the other hand, you might like to maintain the anonymity of the process. This may be met with irritation or frustration at first. The real benefit though, will be if you persist. Students will then come to see the activity as solely about the feedback they have been given and not about the person who has given it.

6) Specific, Relevant, Criteria-Led Targets

Pupils who produce peer-assessments will benefit from the process. This is because they will have:

- Had an opportunity to consider someone else's work. This broadens their understanding and provides them with a further point of reference.
- Had an opportunity to explore the criteria against which their work, and that of their peers, is being judged.

- Had an opportunity to come to a judgement which makes use of the criteria and which, therefore, is predicated on evidence and reasoning.

Pupils who receive peer-assessments will also benefit from the process. This is because they will have:

- Received a judgement which indicates what they have done well and why it is good.
- Received a judgement which does any of the following: indicates how they can improve and why this would be an improvement; indicates a target which they should aim to meet in future work and explains why this will be of benefit; indicates and explains an improvement for the current piece of work and a target for future work.
- Received a judgement which relates clearly and explicitly to the criteria against which their work is being judged.

In an ideal peer-assessment, students will be giving and receiving praise, improvements and targets which are specific, relevant and closely linked to the criteria against which the work is being judged.

Here are three ways to help achieve this:

i.   Make students aware of the criteria they will be judged against before they start their work. This can include: mark schemes, success criteria created by the teacher, success criteria created by students, exemplar pieces of work and general principles (for example, regarding the logical structure of arguments).

ii.   Model the giving of praise and the setting of targets. You might do this with a piece of student work; a piece of exemplar work provided by an exam board; or a piece which you yourself have created.

iii.   Demonstrate what unhelpful feedback looks like ('I love the colours you used!'; 'Really, really nice work'; 'Your presentation is super' and so on) and indicate why it is unhelpful: because it does not help the recipient to learn. You might want to put examples of good and bad peer-assessment feedback on your classroom wall. Alternatively, display it on the board while students go about the task.

7) Three Stars and a Wish

'Three stars and a wish' is a common peer-assessment technique which students can use to give feedback in writing or orally. The three stars refer to the identification of three good things about the work which is being assessed and the wish refers to one thing that could be improved in order to make the work better.

An advantage of this approach is that it couches peer-assessment in language which is both accessible and inherently positive. It is therefore of particular use when one is working with younger students. In such situations it can prove a good means by which to introduce peer-assessment. There is also the benefit that the activity sounds more like a game than what it actually is – the act of marking someone else's work (although perhaps this is just a game anyway – in Wittgenstein's sense at least).

Ask students to read through, watch, look at or listen to the work of their peer. Explain that they should be aiming to identify three things for which they can award 'stars' and that these should be really good things about the work. Indicate that they should also be on the lookout for one thing they wish could be done in the future to make the work even better.

You might like to provide students with a pro-forma they have to fill in. This can include images of three stars and a wand (to represent the wish). Alternatively, and if students are providing the feedback in writing, you can ask them to draw three stars and a wand in their partner's book and to write their comments beside these images.

'Three stars and a wish' is also a good technique to use when something is being performed or presented in front of the class. Before the presentation or performance begins, tell your students that you will be coming to them for three stars and a wish at the end of the show. Another option is to pick out four students in advance and to indicate that you will be asking them specifically for three stars and a wish. A nice aspect of doing peer-assessment in this way is that the pupils who have presented or performed experience a public avowal of what they have done well. They also get the opportunity to respond to the improvement which has been suggested.

One more possibility is to provide the entire audience with a 'three stars and a wish' pro-forma. These can be completed while the presentation or performance takes place. At the end they can be collected-in and given to the performer(s), who can look through them at their leisure.

A final point to note is that you might like to re-name 'three stars and a wish'. Here are some possible alternatives:

- Three goals and a penalty (can you score the penalty next time?)
- Three lions and a cheetah (can you catch the cheetah?)
- Three wins and a draw (can you turn the draw into a win?)

8) Coloured Dots

This activity uses small circular stickers in various colours to provide peer feedback. Such stickers are available cheaply from most stationers. The two great benefits of the approach are that it allows all students to look at a wide range of work and that it provides everyone in the class with some level of positive feedback. Here are three ways to put it into practice:

i. Student work is displayed at the front of the class or left on student desks. Each pupil receives an allocation of coloured dots. They should receive about a third the number of dots as there are students in the class. Pupils are invited to walk around the room and to place their coloured dots on work they think is good. They should write a comment next to their dot, indicating what it is they think is good about the work. There are two rules. First, students are not allowed to give more than two dots to any one piece of work. Second, once a piece of work has X number of dots (the exact number will depend on how many students you have in your class – you will need to calculate what the number should be), it may not receive any more. This ensures that everyone in the class receives positive comments about their work.

ii. Students receive a pro-forma containing a list of adjectives, criteria or statements which can be used to describe work produced in class (for example: innovative, creative, thoughtful, analytical, makes good use of reasons, demonstrates understanding of the text, and so on). They write their name at the top of this pro-forma and place it next to their work, displaying both items on their desks. Each pupil receives an allocation of coloured dots. They should receive about a third the number of dots as there are students in the class. Pupils are invited to walk around the room and to look at the work that is on display. They place their coloured dots on the pro-forma next to the work, choosing the category, statement or criterion they think is most appropriate. There is only one rule: Students are not allowed to place more than one dot on any one pro-forma. This ensures that all students receive praise for their work (and, just to be sure, the teacher can go round with some stickers as well).

iii.   The third option is to run the activity as in (ii) above, but with one alteration. Provide two thirds of the class with stickers of one colour. These are 'strength' stickers. Provide the final third of the class with stickers of another colour. These are 'target' stickers. Students receiving target sticker should be given three each (this means there will be one target sticker per student in the class). Pupils walk around the room and place their stickers on pieces of work, writing their comments next to them. Those who have 'target' stickers are only allowed to place them on work which already has three or more 'strength' stickers. This ensures the requisite balance of strengths to targets (and also means that those with 'target' stickers will chivvy along those with 'strength' stickers if they are being tardy!).

9) Work on Desks

This is a variation on the three approaches outlined in the previous entry – 'Coloured Dots'. It works as follows:

Students display their work on their desks or at the front of the class. The latter is more useful for group work. This is because less work will have been produced and it will therefore be possible to display it all in a smaller space.

The class is divided. If students have been working individually then two thirds are designated as 'strength-identifiers' and one third as 'target-setters'. If students have been working in groups then one or two groups (depending on numbers) are designated as 'target-setters' and the rest as 'strength-identifiers'.

Students walk around the room looking at the work their peers have produced. 'Target-setters' have the job of ensuring that, by the end of the activity, every piece of work has one target written on it. 'Strength-identifiers' have the job of ensuring that, by the end of the activity, every piece of work has at least three strengths written on it.

This approach offers a good contrast to that explained in the 'Coloured Dots' entry. Some students may not like the idea of using the dots; older classes in particular may view it as something which is not sufficiently mature for them (though I have seen it work wonderfully well with adults). In addition, by focussing solely on strengths and targets, without the added diversion of the dots, the method can bring a more orderly and academic sense to proceedings. This can be of particular use when peer-assessing work which relates to examinations or other forms of external assessment.

As ever, it is important to stress to students that the comments they make should be specific, relevant and linked to the assessment criteria. This will ensure that they help the authors of the work to learn and to make progress.

Here are two alternatives, briefly explained, which can also be used:

i.   Give pupils Post-It® notes on which to write their feedback. These can then be stuck onto students' work. This approach is good if there is some reason why writing directly onto student work or in student books would not be welcome – either by yourself or by your pupils.

ii.   Give students a comment sheet which they place beside their work. This should have two boxes, one for strengths and one for a target. The latter box should be smaller so as to ensure a high ratio of strengths to targets.

10) Identify and Show

This entry focusses on the importance of students demonstrating how the improvements and targets they identify can be put into practice. I will outline three reasons as to why this is valuable and then provide five examples demonstrating how to make it happen.

Reasons why it is valuable:

Showing how something can be put into practice makes things clearer for the audience. It is for this reason that we use examples when communicating with one another.

If a student knows they have to demonstrate how a target or an improvement is to be done, it is more likely they will think carefully about it and identify one which is specific and closely tied to the learning.

Doing that which you are advising someone else to do is a good way of assessing whether what you are proposing is realistic or not.

Examples of how you might help students demonstrate improvements and targets:

i.   Model the identification of a target or an improvement and the subsequent demonstration of how to go about achieving this. You could do this with an exemplar piece of work, something produced by a student in a previous year or with a piece of work you have created.

ii.   Set clear parameters to help structure what you are asking students to do. For example: Identify one success criteria which your partner has not met and show them how they could meet it.

iii.   Encourage students to discuss the improvements and targets they have suggested with the person whose work they have assessed. The discussion will give them an opportunity to expand on what they have written and to explain how they see their peer putting the improvement or target into practice.

iv. Ask students to redo a small portion of the work which they have peer-assessed in accordance with the improvement or target they have identified. This can include any sort of work and is not limited to writing.

v. Pick out a student who has successfully identified an improvement or a target in their peer-assessment and then demonstrated to their partner how this could be put into practice. Ask them to recreate the process. They could do this in front of the whole class or they could work with a small group of their peers who you think would benefit from such support.

11) Using Pro-Forma

A pro-forma is a pre-made document which students are given to fill in. I have indicated in some of the previous entries how these might be used. Their great advantage is that they make life easier for students. They provide a clear structure, dictated by the teacher, which pupils can follow. As such, they diminish ambiguity and encourage pupils down paths which the teacher has identified as being of benefit.

You will have to decide what sort of pro-forma is appropriate for your students and for the work which is to be peer-assessed.

A final point to note is that pro-forma can save you time: first, because you can store them on your computer and use them again and again; and second, because once you have shown your students how to use them, you will most likely not need to show them again. This means you can save time in future lessons by using the same pro-forma; pupils will immediately know what it is they are expected to do.

12) Using Mark-Schemes

Coming to terms with a mark-scheme can be a powerful learning experience for a student. It gives them an insight into what they are being judged against and allows them to experience what it is like to be a teacher or an examiner.

All of this is of great benefit: it helps students to conceptualise their work from a less subjective perspective; it allows them to better understand how their work is likely to be interpreted; and it develops their ability to make judgements about what constitutes good work, and vice-versa.

Here are five ways students can use mark-schemes for peer-assessment:

i.   Give students a mark-scheme and ask them to use it to mark the work of their peers. In the case of examination classes, it is usually best to furnish students with the mark-scheme provided by the exam board, unmediated by yourself. While some students may find using this difficult at first, the benefits of coming to terms with it cannot be underestimated. After all, it is that which their work will ultimately be judged against.

ii.   In advance of a piece of work, develop a mark-scheme in conjunction with your students. This should be a collaborative exercise in which all members of the group have the opportunity to contribute. When pupils have completed their work, ask them to get into pairs and to peer-assess what their partner has done using the mark-scheme. It is a good idea to create the mark-scheme in the latter half of one lesson and to then do the task and the peer-assessment in the next lesson. This will give you time in-between to photocopy the mark-scheme you and your class have created.

iii.　Provide students with a simplified version of a mark-scheme which you use. This works well with younger pupils who might not be able to access the language of a formal mark-scheme. By giving them a simplified version you will be allowing them to experience working with something representative of the real thing. You might find it useful to provide bullet points rather than continuous prose.

iv.　Set students an exam question and print off the appropriate piece of the mark-scheme. Enlarge this to A3-size. When students have completed their work, ask them to swap with a partner. Each pair then receives an A3 sheet (ideally the section of the mark scheme will fit on one piece of paper). They begin by reading through and discussing the mark-scheme. Following this they mark their partner's work. Finally, the pairs come back together and exchange feedback, making explicit reference to the mark-scheme as they do.

v.　Spend time with students exploring the relevant mark-scheme before they begin a piece of work. This can include the use of various discussion, comprehension and application activities. The point is to help students develop an understanding of what their work will be judged against and what they will be using to assess the work of their peers.

13) Discussing Peer-Assessments

As has already been intimated, discussing peer-assessments is of great benefit to students. There are two key reasons for this, one concerning form and one concerning content. Taking the latter first, discussion of feedback is a good way for comments to be clarified and for rationales to be made explicit. In terms of form, discussion as a process has been shown to aid student learning and the development of understanding. This occurs thanks to the opportunity which is provided for expression of one's thoughts and the concomitant remoulding which takes place, as a result of processing what the other person in the discussion has said and through personal reflection on the thoughts one has articulated.

Here are three ways to structure discussion of peer-assessments. The benefit of using a specific structure is that it directs student-talk towards the ends which you identify as being important.

i.   Partners take it in turns to talk through the peer-assessments they have given. This should be supported by a series of questions or topic areas displayed on the board which must be covered in their explanations. These could include: Why did you identify those particular strengths? Why are the strengths examples of good things in the work? How did you go about picking out the strengths? Why have you set that particular target or improvement? How will it help your peer to learn? As the student talks through their explanation, their partner should ask questions, make comments and respond to what is said. This will see a discussion develop, one predicated on the explanation given by the first student.

ii.   Partners take it in turns to interview one another. The subject of the interview is the interviewee's thoughts on the work they have assessed and the thinking behind the strengths and targets they have identified. A good way to scaffold this is to come up with a collection of interview questions as a class. Students can then use these to structure their discussions, with the caveat being that, if they wish, they can develop their own questions as well. You might also like to provide a pro-forma on which interviewers can make notes.

iii.   Partners are given a selection of question cards which they draw out at random and then discuss. To make the cards, create a set of questions in a word processing programme. Draw a box around each question. Print the sheet off and stick it onto a piece of card. Cut this up, stack the individual items and then secure them with a rubber band. Each pair is given a set of these cards. The questions should be generic so that they can be used with any peer-assessment. For example: What did you think of the work? What was good about the work and why? How could the work be improved? How do the two pieces of work compare? What did you think about the structure of the work? What could you take from the work and use in the future? How might you combine the best bits of both pieces of work?

14) Self-Peer Comparison

This activity is a good way to get students thinking about perspectives and interpretations. It works as follows:

Ask students to produce a self-assessment of their work but to keep the results of this secret. Students then get into pairs, swap their work and complete a peer-assessment. These are shared and pupils compare what their partner has written with their own self-assessments. Finally, a discussion ensues in which pairs talk about the self- and peer-assessments they have given. Conversations should focus on the similarities and differences which are evident.

The great advantage of this activity is that it presents pupils with a personal and an external perspective on their work. It may be that in some instances these prove to be fairly similar – perhaps even identical. In many cases, however, there are likely to be differences between the two assessments. These may be in terms of the strengths, targets or improvements which have been identified; the overall response to the work; or the way in which it has been understood by the assessor.

Through discussion, the causes of these differences can be drawn out and made plain. It may be that students will disagree with one another. Do not be too concerned if this happens. It is likely to have a positive effect as it will stimulate pupils into defending the assessments they have made. This will result in them marshalling reasons, evidence and examples in order to support their own arguments (the assessments they have made are arguments – they are conclusions made on the basis of evidence).

In order to encourage students to think carefully about the differences between their self-assessments and the peer-assessments their partners have created, build some reflection time into the activity. This may take the form of a couple of minutes in-between the returning of the peer-assessments and the beginning of the discussion, in which students think in silence about what has been written and make some notes in response (or write some questions they would like to put to their partner, perhaps ones which seek clarification or which contest what has been said).

By delineating a period of time in which students have to reflect, you will be stressing the importance to them of considering the implications of the differences in the assessments. In addition, it will help them to understand how texts are open to multiple interpretations – not all of which will agree.

Here is one final thought. You might like to create a pro-forma for this task. It could be as simple as an A4-sheet divided in half. Students complete their self-assessment on the top half of their sheet, fold this over so that it is hidden, and pass the paper on to their partner. They, in turn, complete their peer-assessment on the bottom half of the sheet. When the pro-forma is returned, students open them up and compare the two assessments.

A nice aspect of this approach is its theatricality. Opening the sheet up to its full size, and revealing the two assessments, side-by-side, is mildly dramatic, adding a little excitement to the activity.

15) Read Aloud and Peer-Assess

There is a qualitative difference between writing and speech. While each makes use of the same language and many of the same conventions, the structures which underpin them are fundamentally different. Here are some of the disparities:

Writing – Permanent; fixed; unresponsive to the audience; usually devoid of supplements; time-consuming to correct or alter.

Speech – Impermanent (unless recorded); disappears on being uttered; highly responsive to the audience; always supplemented (by tone, inflexion, gestures and so on); easy to correct or alter.

This indicates why discussion is an important part of classroom practice. It also suggests why it might be useful to give students the opportunity to talk before they begin a written piece of work.

This particular activity makes use of the differences between writing speech as well as one aspect of their interaction. It works as follows:

Students work in pairs or threes. They take it in turns to read their work aloud. While they do this, the other members of the group listen. The student then reads their work aloud for a second time. Other group members listen and make notes. A minute or two is given in which students can gather their thoughts. An oral peer-assessment follows, with this leading into a discussion between the assessor(s) and the student being assessed. The process is repeated until each member of the group has had their work peer-assessed.

The strengths of this activity are as follows:

- When reading aloud, students will have to think carefully about whether their work makes sense and how it attempts to convey meaning. Both of these elements can be easily overlooked when pupils are looking at or scanning their work.
- The student(s) doing the peer-assessment will have to pay close attention to what their partner is saying. This promotes careful, active listening.
- The oral peer-assessment promotes discussion and gives all parties an opportunity to edit and develop their thoughts as well as to respond to the thoughts or others.

16) Silent Debate Peer-Assessment

Silent debate works as follows:

Four to five large sheets of paper are distributed through the room. Each has a question or statement related to the topic written in the middle of it. Students walk around the room in silence. They make comments on the sheets of paper. When they have finished, they continue to walk around except they now make comments on what other people have written. At the end of the activity, groups or the whole class discuss some of the comments which have been made.

Silent debate peer-assessment works as follows:

As above, except in place of questions or statements insert anonymous work, or work that you have kept over from the previous year. The comments which students make are identifications of strengths, areas for improvement and targets. At the end of the activity, discuss certain comments as a whole class or give each large sheet of paper to a different group and ask them to analyse what has been written and to feed this back to the whole class.

This activity has a number of advantages:

- It provides students with an opportunity to peer-assess a number of pieces of work. This widens their range of reference points, making it easier for them to think about what makes a good piece of work in relation to the present topic.
- Students have the chance to read a number of other people's peer-assessments. This will give them with a wide range of ideas. It will also help them to refine their own peer-assessments by providing examples to which they can compare the evaluations they have made.
- By using anonymous work, or work produced by students during the previous year, the activity depersonalises the peer-assessment process. This means that students are solely focussed on the peer-assessment (and, therefore, an analysis of the work in relation to criteria in order to reach a judgement). This makes the activity particularly good for honing peer-assessment skills and learning from mistakes.

A further possibility you might like to pursue, which extends and develops the activity, works as follows:

At the conclusion of the silent debate, divide the class into the same number of groups as there are large sheets of paper (you will need to think ahead here to ensure you do not end up with oversized groups). Give each group one of the sheets of paper. Ask them to analyse the peer-assessments and to pick out what they think are the three most compelling targets or improvements. Having done this, the group should redo the original piece of work, taking account of the targets and improvements on which they have settled. Conclude the activity by having groups present their new pieces of work to one another.

17) Multiple Peer-Assessments

Having the same piece of work peer-assessed a number of times can be of major benefit to students. There are two main reasons for this. First, it results in them receiving a range of feedback which, while perhaps overlapping at times, is likely to contain a number of different perspectives on their work. Second, it gives them an opportunity to analyse the different ways in which the work they have created might be received by others. Seeing as all the communication we do in the classroom, in whatever form, is by necessity intended to convey meaning to others, the opportunity to assess whether one has communicated successfully what one intended is particularly useful.

Students also benefit from the process of completing a series of peer-assessments. Again, there are two main reasons for this. First, repetition leads to mastery. Of course, your students will be close to mastering peer-assessment anyway because of how it is embedded in your lessons. Nonetheless, the quick succession of repeated peer-assessments which this activity involves will help accelerate (or reinforce) their skills. Second, analysing and evaluating a number of pieces of work, rather than just one, gives students the chance to expand their knowledge of what constitutes work (of varying standards) in the particular topic being studied. They will therefore have a wider range of reference points against which to judge their own work.

Here are three ways in which you might structure multiple peer-assessments:

i.   Students are put into groups of four. Each student peer-assesses the work produced by the other members of their group. Strengths and targets are written in student books or on a pro-forma. When the peer-assessments have been completed, comments are returned to the author of the work and a discussion ensues.

ii. Students are given a pro-forma which contains space for nine strengths and three targets or improvements. Everyone stands up and walks around the room. Pupils must find three people to peer-assess their work and to fill in their pro-forma.

iii. Half the class remain sat down and the other half stand up. Those who are sat down must display their work on their desks in front of them. Those who are stood up must walk around and peer-assess the work of three people who are sat down. Assessments should include discussion and questioning between the student who is sat down and the student who is stood up. When all this has been done, the two halves of the class swap over.

18) What Are Criteria?

When first introducing peer-assessment to students, it is worth exploring the idea of criteria with them. This affords an entry point into the nature of assessment and the logical function which underpins it.

Consider some examples which make the point:

- When you mark a student's book you refer to criteria which you have internalised in the course of your professional life. These include general and specific criteria as well as examples of work you have previously marked.

- When someone asks you if you like something, the response you give is in reference to something else. In order to like something, there must be things about it which you like. Therefore, you are referencing what it is, what it does or how it makes you feel against some prior knowledge – the knowledge of what you like, how you like feeling and so on.
- At the end of a driving test the examiner turns to you and tells you whether you have passed or not. They do so by referring to the check-sheet they have been filling-in during the test. This presents a set of criteria including minor and major errors. A certain number or combination of these leads to a failure. In addition, the examiner has been referring to his or her experience, knowledge and understanding while you have been driving, in order to judge whether what you have done is commensurate with any of the errors indicated on the check-sheet.

Criteria underpin judgement. By spending time discussing this with students, you will be helping them to get a better handle on peer-assessment (and self-assessment as well).

One game you can use involves asking students to draw a house and then revealing the assessment criteria after they have drawn it (for example: 5 points for a chimney; 2 points for a front door). This quickly demonstrates the difficulty of making accurate judgements if one is not aware of the criteria one is supposed to be using.

19) Specific Focus

In many cases, peer-assessments will be concerned with the application of a mark-scheme or with the referencing of a set of criteria. These are both general endeavours based on things which apply across the board, regardless of whose work is being assessed. There is much to commend such an approach. It replicates what takes place in externally-assessed examinations and is also indicative of much of life as a whole. If one goes into a profession there is likely to be a code of conduct or a set of standards against which one's work will be judged. If one makes an application for something, it is likely there will be a set of criteria against which all applications are evaluated.

On occasion, however, it can be fruitful to deviate from this familiar path and to encourage students to specify what it is they want the peer-assessment of their work to be about. Asking a partner to maintain a specific focus leads to certain benefits which are difficult to achieve elsewhere.

First, it encourages students to think critically about their own learning. If they are to designate an area of focus for their peer, they must look in detail at what they themselves have done and where exactly it is they are at. In effect, pupils will be doing a self-diagnosis. They will be analysing themselves in order to identify something which would benefit from another person's perspective.

Second, it gives students an opportunity, when they are doing their peer-assessments, to consider an aspect of learning which they hitherto may have neglected. Being asked to focus on a specific area which someone else has chosen causes pupils to think about that area and to reflect on it in light of their own work, as well as that of their peer.

A good way to go about a peer-assessment in which students choose a specific focus is as follows:

Before students begin their work, ask them to reflect on their recent learning. They should identify what they have been doing well and what they have been struggling with. Next, they should choose something they believe it would be helpful to focus on developing through the present piece of work.

When students have completed their work, put them into pairs. Ask them to swap what they have produced and to explain to each other what it was they chose to focus on. Indicate that pupils, when conducting their peer-assessments, should focus on the same thing. The assessments take place and are followed by paired discussion.

20) Random Peer-Assessment

The final activity in this section is similar to the previous entry in that it asks students to focus on a specific thing in their peer-assessments. It differs, however, because that thing is chosen at random. There are three key benefits. First, the whole class focuses on the same aspect in their peer-assessments. This means that subsequent discussions will be informed by a shared knowledge and understanding, leading to talk which is richer and more purposeful. Second, students are compelled to focus on aspects of their peers' work which they might previously have ignored, or perhaps never even have thought about. Third, the activity has a sense of drama – what will be picked out? The teacher can play this up in order to engage and motivate students.

Here are five ways in which to randomise your peer-assessments:

i.   Cut up a selection of success criteria so that each one is on a separate strip of paper. Put all of these in a hat and pull one out (or ask a student to pull one out) at random.

ii.   Write a range of assessment objectives on bits of card and shuffle these. Invite a student to select one at random.

iii.   Write six aspects of learning on the board and number these. Roll a die (or ask a student to) in order to select which particular aspect pupils will base their peer-assessments around.

iv. Create a PowerPoint presentation. Write a different success criterion on each slide. Change the transition speed to '0' and loop the slideshow. Press play and then ask a student to shout out the word: 'Stop!' At that point, press escape to stop the slideshow. Pupils focus on the success criterion which is on display in their peer-assessments.

v. Secretly assign a range of assessment objectives to letters of the alphabet. Use a continuous run of letters, such as A-H. Ask a student to select a letter from the range. Whatever assessment objective has been assigned to that letter is the one which the class will focus on.

Chapter Six - Self-Assessment

Self-assessment opens up the assessment process for students. It gives them an opportunity to use criteria in order to make judgements. In addition, it encourages them to identify strengths and set targets which make use of those criteria. It thus helps pupils to better understand what their own work is being judged against, what good work ought to include, and how to go about making their own work better. The final point to note is that self-assessment encourages students to look at what they have produced from critical and developmental perspectives. It therefore helps them to think about learning as a process, one in which everyone can achieve success and make progress.

In this chapter there are twelve different entries. Each one explains an approach to self-assessment, one or more activities you might use to structure self-assessment, or some part of self-assessment which is worthy of close attention.

Everything has a practical focus and can be used in any subject with any age-group.

1) Criteria Variations

As has been stressed elsewhere in the book, any judgement takes place in relation to some set of criteria. In everyday life this can be a multitude of things. In the classroom it is likely to be something linked to learning. This might be subject-specific or generic. The three most common sets of criteria used to make judgements are mark-schemes, success criteria and past performance. The latter is best conceptualised as whether or not a target has been achieved (the alternative is to judge whether a standard has been maintained. You may find this useful but, for me, it does not have much to do either with learning or with making progress).

The more students are aware of that which they are judging their work against, the more accurate and precise their evaluations are likely to be. In addition, a better knowledge of assessment criteria will probably lead to a better quality of work. This is because students will know what it is they ought to do in order to achieve highly.

When we consider criteria, we must not think only of their content. There is also the matter of the conventions which permeate such reference points. Think back to the first time that you used a mark-scheme as a teacher. If you have taught more than one subject, consider how you felt when you first encountered a mark-scheme used in a subject that was new to you. Both experiences can be jarring. There is jargon to penetrate. One must come to terms with the medium through which the language is being conveyed, as well as the language itself.

As teachers, this is something with which we are familiar. Throughout a child's schooling they are being taught both content and form. For example, a ten year-old learning about science is not only learning about the nature of the world as science reveals it to us; they are also learning about how science looks at the world and how it then presents its findings. Skipping forward, consider how an eighteen year-old studying English, History and Physics comes to understand that each subject possesses its own conventions for the communication of information and understanding. This is on top of – or as well as – the content and conceptual apparatus which is specific to each of the disciplines.

Returning to the issue of criteria, the point is that, as teachers, we have extensive experience in teaching students how to read and understand different genres (in the broad sense). Mark-schemes and the like should be seen as simply another form of writing to deal with in this way. What follows is a collection of nine activities you can use to help students come to terms with various sets of criteria, such that they might be able to assess their own work with confidence and skill.

A) Mark-Schemes

First Method: Before beginning a piece of work, give students a copy of the mark-scheme against which it will be assessed and a highlighter pen. Ask pupils to read through and to highlight any words or phrases which they do not understand. Indicate that they should err on the side of caution. It is better to highlight more and to have your beliefs confirmed than it is to highlight less and retain misconceptions.

When this has been done you have two options. On the one hand, you can invite students to discuss what they have highlighted with their peers. They will work together to try and unravel any uncertainties and will help one another to develop understanding. On the other hand, you can lead the class in a group discussion in which you invite pupils to propose the terms or words which ought to be discussed.

Second Method: Hand out a mark-scheme to students. Put pupils into groups and assign each group a section of the mark-scheme. Ask groups to decode and then rewrite the mark-scheme so that it is accessible for everybody in the class. The rewriting could involve a full revision, minor changes, a supplementary summary or an annotated revision in which difficult phrases or words are accompanied by explanatory notes.

Third Method: In advance of the lesson, print off a set of mark-schemes. There should be enough for one per group. Cut these up into manageable sections. In the lesson, divide the class into groups. Explain that each group will be working through the mark-scheme at their own pace. The intention is to ensure that all students come to feel at ease with the documents structure and content.

Begin by giving each group the first part of the mark-scheme. They should analyse and discuss this. When the group are confident they understand that part of the mark-scheme, they should send one member up to the front to collect the next section. This process is repeated until each group has analysed and discussed each section of the mark scheme. If one group finishes earlier than the others, ask them to summarise each section, to create a list of the overall aims of the mark-scheme, or to split up and go and help other groups with their analyses and discussions.

B) Success Criteria

First Method: Certain themes run through the work students are asked to do during any year of their school life (and, indeed, across the years). For example, a twelve year-old student might be expected to do the following in all of their subjects: support any claims made with reasons, examples or evidence; think carefully about what words accurately express what is meant; answer questions or do what tasks ask.

Identify general success criteria that apply to the age-group you are teaching. Display these in your room and discuss them with your students. Show them pieces of work which exemplify each of the success criteria. Place these on display with a summary of why they are good. For each piece of work you ask students to do, provide (or agree upon) some specific success criteria. Stress that these are a supplement to the general criteria, not a replacement.

Second Method: Work with your class to develop success criteria. These could be general success criteria for use across a unit of work or across a year, or specific success criteria tied to the task in hand. You might like to use a discussion technique such as snowballing, think-pair-share or envoys in order to structure the task.

There are two main advantages of approaching success criteria in this way. First, by having students think about what criteria might be appropriate, you will be encouraging them to look carefully at the nature of assessment and what, in this case, it should entail.

Second, by creating criteria in collaboration with students, you will be promoting a cooperative atmosphere and encouraging them to feel ownership over the material. This, in turn, will lead to increased motivation.

To extend this approach, do as follows: Once you have agreed on a set of success criteria with your class, divide these up and assign each one to a different group of students. Ask groups to come up with an example which shows their success criterion in action. These examples can then be shared with the class (and put on display). The purpose of this development is to further scaffold the success criteria for students through modelling what good work out to look like.

Third Method: Put students into groups of three or four. Ask them to create a television advertisement 'selling' the success criteria. This should be about thirty seconds long and should focus on explaining what the success criteria are and why they are important. It should also give examples of how one might go about meeting them.

This activity sees students actively engaging with the criteria. They will be analysing the material and then manipulating it in order to create something in which it forms an essential part (the television advert). As such, they should develop a good understanding of the criteria and what it will mean to meet them. Of course, the activity is a lot of fun as well.

C) Personal Targets

First Method: This activity is best used with younger students. It encourages them to visualise themselves meeting their target. It is appropriate whether the target has been set by the teacher, by a peer or by the student themselves. It works as follows:

Explain to your class that one of the best ways to meet a target is to think about the small steps you can take to get there. Point out that one can cover a distance in a series of small steps which would be impossible to cover in a single leap. You might like to use the analogy of athletics. World record breakers do not transform their times overnight. They engage in a long series of small steps (also called training!) in order to reach the target they have set for themselves. Without the small steps, they would not be able to cover the large distance between where they were at and where they wanted to be.

Ask your class to think about the small steps they will need to take in order to meet their targets. Encourage them to identify three and to then visualise these through a poster or a cartoon strip. Indicate that the conclusion of their work should show them successfully meeting (or surpassing) their targets.

Second Method: When students have been given a target, either by themselves, a peer or a teacher, ask them to compare this with three other people in the class. Explain that the purpose is to discuss the similarities and the differences between the targets. In doing this, students will be compelled to think carefully about what their targets mean. The act of comparison helps one to develop a better understanding of both objects in question. The attachments students will have to their own targets (because of their relevance) should lead to a disproportionate development in their understanding of these, through the comparison process. This is what we as teachers want.

You might like to provide pupils with some questions to help guide their comparisons. These will encourage them to look at and think about different aspects of their targets. For example: What would you say is the main difference between your target and your peer's target? What similarities can you identify between the two targets? How might the results of meeting your targets be different? What different things will you both have to do in order to meet your targets? How might you explain the differences between the targets to someone outside of school?

Third Method: It is important to explain or to demonstrate how an improvement can be made or how a target can be met. Learning ought not to be a guessing a game. With that said, I appreciate how the demands on a teacher's time may militate against appending explanations or demonstrations to every piece of formative feedback. In addition, if a student has set themselves a target through self-assessment, it is likely that they will not, as yet, be completely confident in how to go about achieving it. This activity provides an alternative approach. It works as follows:

Students have been given a target, either by themselves, a peer, or the teacher. They are asked to reflect on this for a couple of minutes and to consider how they might go about meeting it. Next, the class is invited to stand up and to walk around the room. Students are asked to find a peer who can do their target for them. They should speak to a range of people, sharing their target and asking if they can demonstrate or explain how it might be met. The teacher should ensure they themselves are available and invite students to come to them as well as to go to their peers.

This activity is premised on the fact that in any one class of students, it is likely that there will be a range of targets and strengths. It is therefore probable that all students will be able to find someone who has the skills and understanding to demonstrate or exemplify the successful meeting of their target. The teacher is included as a person to talk to so that, if someone struggles to find a peer who can help them with their target, there is a fall-back option – a failsafe, if you will.

2) Identifying Strengths

I have found it to be the case in teaching, and in life in general, that many people struggle to identify their own strengths. From my experience I believe this is due to psychological and cultural factors rather than any deficit of analytical ability.

If students are to benefit from self-assessments, they need to be confident in identifying their own strengths and in justifying the judgements which underpin these. I will look briefly at the obstacles I mentioned above before going on to offer some activities you might use to help your pupils.

Two psychological issues are worth mentioning. First are the difficulties inherent in reflecting on one's own thoughts and actions, as well as the work one produces. This is particularly the case when you are younger. As time rolls on and experience accrues, it becomes easier to introspect in the light of what has happened previously. This is a significant component of what we call wisdom.

Our experience of the world is total – it is everything that we encounter; nothing more and nothing less. Yet this experience is at the same time partial, for it is what we encounter, not what anyone else encounters. For proof of this we need only look at how two separate individuals might interpret the same rule in completely different ways. I am not contending that there is no objective reality, just that we all have a separate experience of it.

In terms of identifying strengths, this can make it difficult for individuals to analyse those things which go to make up a part of who and what they are – the things they do, say and create. It is not easy to look disinterestedly at that which composes a significant part of our experience.

The second issue to mention is closely related. It is the identification of what we do, how we act and what we produce with our conceptualisation of our selves. David Hume noted that when we look inside ourselves there is not a single thing that we can fix upon and say: 'Yes – that is I'. Instead, he suggests there are many separate things which in conjunction we label as ourselves. These are things such as experiences, memories, thoughts, ideas and so on. We do not need to go any further into this here. The point I want to make is that we consider ourselves to be made up of, or at least partly constituted by, many different things.

Take this book as an example. I have written it and you are reading it. For you, it is an external object; something which you are assimilating but which is being filtered through your own mind. I imagine (though do not know) that you are reading it with a view to developing your understanding of assessment for learning and that, as you go about reading it, you are picking out what you agree with or what you are prepared to accept and rejecting or questioning other things. For me, the book is an internal and an external object. It is internal in as much as it is a representation of things I have thought (and that I continue to think); it is a product of my mind. It is external because it represents a realisation of my thoughts in a physical form – one which is transferable and can be shared by other people.

In the context of one's notion of oneself, this book is likely to play little to no part for you and a somewhat larger part for me. It is something which I identify with my own self – it is one of the many things which go to make up my self. For you, the experience of reading and using it is much less significant (and probably involves a good deal less time than the writing of it).

Transfer this argument to the classroom and we can see that a student's relationship to their own work, thoughts, actions and so on is likely to be qualitatively different to the relationship we have with them. It is important to help pupils to put the emotional reactions which can be a consequence of their being asked to engage analytically with a part of themselves to one side. The stress must be on learning as a developmental process in which everyone is engaged. Self-assessment must be seen as a way to coach oneself. It is not about the rightness and wrongness of one's work, thoughts or actions, but about why it is good and how it can be made better.

The final factor to consider regarding students' difficulties in identifying strengths is cultural. I have grown up and worked only in the United Kingdom and, while the comments which follow may be transferable to other cultures, they are made solely with reference to my own experience.

There is a tendency for individuals to refrain from stressing good things that they have done or good aspects of their characters. I think there are a number of explanations for this. First is the desire that others do not take offence; many feel that to talk about one's strengths implies arrogance. This is because it can suggest self-absorption and because it can call up connotations of competition (in the sense that to be good at something is often contextualised as being better than someone else). Second is the fear of being challenged to justify what one might say about one's strengths. Third is the underlying moral maxim that to talk about something good connected to oneself is to devalue it. I would suggest that this links to ideas such as those articulated in the Christian contention about charity (the left hand should not know what the right hand is doing) and Kant's arguments regarding duty. I would also suggest that the feelings which gave rise to these are to be found in many religious traditions and that they underpin the senses of selflessness, love and justice which are shown as great goods to which we should all aspire.

This is not the place to argue for or against these points. It is, however, the place in which to provide some means whereby we as teachers might surmount or circumvent them in relation to self-assessment. As such, here are five activities you might like to use to help students identify their own strengths:

    i.   **Create a strengths bank.** Divide the class into groups. Explain that the purpose of the activity is to identify as many strengths as possible which are connected to the subject you are teaching. These can be both general and specific. Ask the groups to come up with a list which is as big as possible, or divide the work up and provide each group with a different area on which to focus. When sufficient time has passed, ask groups to share their ideas. This could be through whole-class feedback, group presentations or the use of envoys. Collate the strengths and either display these prominently in your room or give each student a copy to keep in their books. The strengths bank can then be used by students when they are completing self-assessments.

ii.   **Create a strengths bank – part two.** Engage students in a peer-assessment task. Ask them to identify three strengths and one target relevant to the work of their peer. At the end of the activity, charge two or three students (depending on the total number of pupils in your class) with the task of going round the room and recording every class member's strengths. The teacher can then collate these and create a document for students to use in future self-assessments.

iii.   **Exemplar work.** Put students in groups of two or three. Give each group a piece of exemplar work and ask them to identify ten (or fifteen, or twenty) strengths. Explain that the activity is a race and the first team to come up with their list of strengths should signal as soon as they have finished. This list is then read out to the class. Students listen carefully and are allowed to challenge any strength with which they do not agree. Challenges should ask for a justification of why that is a strength and where it can be seen in the exemplar work. Later on in the same lesson (or in the following lesson), students are asked to do a self-assessment. They are encouraged to use the work they did in the activity to help them identify their own strengths.

iv.   **Model self-assessment.** The teacher produces a piece of work and then models a self-assessment in front of the whole class. This includes the identification of strengths and of a target for improvement. The teacher should talk about the mental processes they are using in order to make their judgements. For example, this might include an explanation of what criteria are being called on to decide whether something is a strength or not, or the reasoning process which leads them to settle on three particular strengths rather than on any others.

v.   **Decide on the criteria.** We have spoken at other points about how important criteria or reference points are in relation to the process of judgement. This applies when one is doing self-assessments. Provide success criteria or a mark-scheme which students can use to assess their work. Alternatively, in between the task being completed and the self-assessment, discuss with your class what criteria they could use to judge what they have done. You might like to do this by asking them to think about how they would know if a piece of work was good, or how they would be able to tell what part of a piece of work was the best bit.

You will notice that all these activities scaffold the process of identifying strengths for students. They take pupils a little further than they might be able to go on their own. There are two other general points you might like to consider, both of which link to students being able to identify strengths successfully.

First, create a warm and supportive atmosphere in which learning is seen as an inalienable good and in which it is taken as read that everybody can improve and everybody can develop. I know that you do this anyway, but it is worth mentioning here as such an environment will make it easier for students to feel they can identify their own strengths. This is in part because it will help to dispel some of those inhibiting factors mentioned above.

Second, practice makes perfect. The more students practice identifying strengths, the better they will get. Look to the medium-term and accept that initially the results may not be quite what you want.

3) Setting Oneself Targets

Here are five ways in which you can facilitate your students' setting of personal targets:

i.   **Create a targets bank.** This works in exactly the same way as the strengths bank detailed in the previous entry.

ii.   **Provide students with a sheet they can use to keep track of their targets.** This could be a simple pro-forma they stick in the front of their books. It should provide space for them to write their targets as well as space for them to write about how they have met their targets and where the evidence can be found. You might also like to leave room for them to write down their strengths as well.

iii.   **Provide students with a mark-scheme and ask them to identify where they would like to be in relation to it.** Ask them to analyse the mark-scheme so as to identify a range of targets they will have to meet in order to reach their desired goal. They should then work through these targets one-by-one. Each time they move on, they must be sure they have evidence showing how they have met the last target.

iv. **Set up a discussion activity in which students talk to one another about the targets they are planning to set for themselves.** This could involve pupils working in pairs, threes or slightly larger groups. Stress that this is not a peer-assessment. Rather, it is a self-assessment supplemented by discussion. The purpose is twofold. First, it gives students a chance to articulate their targets. This will help them to refine these and to think about them more carefully. Second, it allows students to share their thoughts with their peers and to receive feedback. Listening to another perspective will help students to reflect on their own ideas. It may also cause them to alter their approach or to take account of something they themselves had not considered.

v. **Give students a selection of categories and ask them to select one from which to set a target.** Categories might include things such as the following: structure; punctuation and spelling; answering the question; creativity; planning; or language. The subject or topic you are teaching will dictate which categories are most appropriate. I would suggest that it is better to make categories broad rather than specific as this presents students with a greater range of options. With that said, you might like to provide a couple of exemplar targets for each category in order to point students in the right direction.

4) Creating Success Criteria

As has been indicated, success criteria are of great relevance to self-assessment. If students know what it is they are to be assessed against, they are more likely to produce work which meets those demands. Also, having formalised terms of reference makes it easier for students to identify strengths, improvements and targets in relation to their own work. Here are three activities through which you can develop success criteria with your students:

Method One: Before beginning a task, divide the class into the same number of groups as success criteria you want (so, if you want five success criteria then divide the class into five groups). Explain that each group has to agree on one success criterion which they believe it will be important for students to try and meet in their work. If you are concerned about different groups coming up with the same criteria, give each group a different category from which they must develop a success criterion. This will minimise the possibility of repetition.

After sufficient time has passed, ask the groups to select a representative who will share their success criterion with the class. Go round the representatives in turn. They should state their group's criterion, explain why they have chosen it and suggest an example of what work which has met it might look like (indicate in advance that this will be expected from each group). The teacher should record the success criteria on the board so that students can refer to them when they begin their work.

Method Two: Provide students with a list of nine success criteria. Explain that they will be working in pairs and that their task is to order these criteria into a 'diamond nine'. This involves one item being placed at the top, two underneath this, three in the middle, two beneath these and one at the bottom. The position of the criteria in the 'diamond nine' reflects how important students think them to be. That which they view as most important will go at the top. That which they view as least important will go at the bottom.

When pairs have agreed upon their diamond nines, ask them to create a group of four with another pair. The groups should compare their ordering of criteria and discuss the reasons behind their choices. The teacher should then announce that each group must agree on two success criteria they would be happy to put forward to the whole class. Each group in turn shares their choices and the teacher collates the responses.

If a total of between three and five different success criteria are put forward, use these for the task and set students off working. If more than five are put forward, ask the class to vote for the one they would most like to be removed. Repeat this until you pare the results down to five criteria. Any more than this and using them becomes difficult and time-consuming.

Method Three: Introduce students to a task and then display a range of possible success criteria on the board. Give each student a couple of Post-It® notes. Ask them to choose which two success criteria they think are most appropriate for the activity. They should write their reasons for their choices on their Post-It® notes and then go and stick these on the board, on the criteria they have chosen. The teacher counts the votes and indicates what the success criteria will be. They should also share some of the rationales students have given for their choices. If too many success criteria gain enough votes to be put through, use the elimination method outlined above.

5) Redo, Redraft and Rewrite

There are many times when it can be beneficial to ask students to look back over their work and to alter it in some way. Personally, I tend to use this approach if certain students have finished a task on which the rest of the class is still working, or when there is a natural moment for the whole class to look again at a piece of work they have done (for example, at the beginning of a lesson).

Revisiting work encourages students to look critically at that which they have produced. It helps them to see what they do as open to development rather than as something final and fixed. Here are three ways to structure such review-style activities:

Method One: Redo a section of your work. This involves asking students to identify one part of their work which they feel could be improved. Students should first think about what might constitute an improvement for the particular piece of work and then go through and analyse what they have done. It may be that they choose a piece of their work which they feel is below par. Alternatively, it could a section which they feel is good but which they know they are capable of making much better.

When students have identified the section they are going to redo, they should make a note of why they think it needs improving, how precisely they intend to improve it and why this change will constitute something which is better. You might like to discuss this with students or to invite them to share it with the person sat next to them. Finally, students put their improvements into action.

Method Two: Redraft what you have written. This involves asking students to look at a piece of writing they have done and to edit it from top-to-bottom. They should aim to create a new piece of writing which is a clear development of the first piece. This could be in terms of clarity, accuracy, use of language or another reference point.

When it comes to redrafting, it can be useful to share a painting analogy with pupils. Many artists produce sketches which they then develop into a final piece of work. The sketches represent their first attempts at realising what they think and feel about that which is in front of them or that which is in their heads. As such, they put a lot of effort in and try to make their sketches as near to what they want as possible. Nonetheless, when it comes to the final piece of work, the sketches are quickly relegated to a junior role. They become a point on a journey in which the painting is the culmination.

Using this to explain redrafting can help make students feel more at ease with the process of creating a further piece of work. The logic at play can soothe some of the tension which may develop when you ask for a top-to-toe reworking.

Method Three: Rewrite according to X. This activity is only slightly removed from the previous two. Ask students to identify one success criteria or one element of the mark-scheme that they have not successfully put into practice in their writing. When they have done this, they should choose one or more sections of their work to which this applies and rewrite these accordingly.

6) Speaking, Punctuation and Sense (SPS)

This is a great approach to self-assessment which helps students to develop their reading and writing skills. It was introduced to me by a talented colleague at my last school. It works as follows:

When a student indicates that they have finished the task in hand, ask them to 'SPS' their work. As indicated above, the letters refer to spelling, punctuation and sense. Students should look back over what they have done and first check that all the spelling is correct. If they notice any errors, they should write 'Sp' in the margin of their work and make the appropriate corrections. They then look through their work a second time and focus on whether they have used punctuation correctly. If they find any errors, they should write 'P' in the margin and make the appropriate corrections. Finally, students look through their work a third time. They are now checking whether what they have written makes sense. If they find any sentences or paragraphs which do not, they should write 'Se' in the margin and then make the necessary corrections. When students have checked their work for 'SPS', they can discuss the changes they have made with the teacher.

For me, this method has three major benefits.

First, it slows students down. Frequently, pupils labour under the assumption that they should be aiming to complete their work as quickly as is possible. As adults, we can appreciate that this approach is not ideal. What is better is to complete the work in good time while paying close attention to its quality. SPS ensures that students who work (perhaps too) quickly are made to look again at what they have done. The assessment is, in some respects, akin to a reflection. It helps pupils to develop an understanding of why haste is not, in this context, something which one should aim for.

Second, it encourages students to focus closely on what they have written. An unstructured self-assessment may cause pupils to glance over their work or to look at it less critically than they ought to. The specific structure of SPS means that students are compelled to look closely at everything they have written – and to do so three times.

Third, the delineation of the assessment into three separate categories – spelling, punctuation and sense – helps to develop students' understanding of what they ought to be considering when looking at their own work. The criteria of reference are made plain. Further, because the criteria are broken down into three separate elements, they are easier for students to get to grips with (and to remember).

7) Paying Close Attention

The previous two entries have both been concerned with encouraging students to look closely at what they have written so as to work out how to improve it. This entry provides three further ways in which you might ask students to structure such self-assessments. In contrast to SPS, the activities are a little more challenging. You will need to judge where your own students are at before deciding which methods may be best suited to helping them to learn.

Method One: Line-by-line assessment. While this process may be laborious it can yield significant results. It involves students going through their work line-by-line and identifying anything which could be improved or altered. They should make a list as they go along. When finished, they should read through their list and group together similar improvements and alterations. Finally, they should choose the one thing which they feel is most pressing and set this as their target for improvement.

You might support students in this process by providing a range of things they could look for as they go through their work. This might include the following: correct use of key terms; correct spelling of key terms; accurate use of punctuation; logical sentence structure; sentences which clearly connect to one another, and so on.

Method Two: Copy-editing. This is a job which people are employed to do for publishing companies and newspapers. The individuals read through text provided by authors and aim to improve it, ready for publication. Introduce students to the five C's of copy-editing: clear, correct, concise, complete and consistent. Ask them to go through their work and to check that each 'c-word' could be accurately applied to all that they have written. If this is not the case, ask pupils to make the necessary alterations.

Method Three: Read aloud and alter. As has been noted elsewhere, reading something aloud is a powerful way to assess it. The process takes no prisoners. This is unlike the written word, where sentences that don't quite make sense can be glossed over and their meaning inferred. If you are reading such a sentence aloud, this is no longer an option; it just sounds wrong!

When students have finished their work, ask them to read it aloud to themselves. They should annotate their writing, making a note of words, sentences or paragraphs that require improvement. They should continue to improve and re-assess their work until they can read it through in full without being able to identify any errors.

8) Highlighting

Highlighter pens are a great tool students can use when completing self-assessments. Here are three activities you might like to try:

Method One: Provide students with a mark-scheme for the work they have completed and three highlighter pens, each of which should be a different colour. Ask them to use the pens to highlight the parts of the mark-scheme they have successfully achieved and the parts of their work which provide evidence for this.

The result will be a mark-scheme and a piece of work highlighted in parallel colours. For example: if the mark-scheme says that students should demonstrate good knowledge and understanding, the student might highlight this in yellow and then highlight examples in their work of where they have shown good knowledge and understanding.

At the end of the activity the student will be able to see in an arresting visual manner the many things they have achieved. It will also be clear which bits of the mark scheme they have not yet met. This will help them to set an appropriate target for improvement.

Method Two: Before students begin a piece of work, ask them to write out their current target. When the task has been completed, hand out highlighter pens and ask pupils to make a thick dot next to their target. They should then go through their work and highlight where they have met their target. If a student can find little to highlight then they will need to think carefully about whether they understand their target and whether they understand how to put it into practice.

Method Three: When students have finished a piece of work, give them two highlighter pens. Explain that one is the 'strengths pen' and that one is the 'target pen'. Students should go through their work and first highlight three good things they have done. Underneath, they should write out what each one of these is and why they represent something good.

Next, students should go through and highlight one thing in their work which could be improved. They should then write this out underneath, explain why it needs to be improved and indicate what they will do next time to secure such an improvement.

This activity helps students to connect their strengths and targets with specific aspects of their work. It also provides positive reinforcement. This is because it clearly shows strengths outnumbering areas for improvement. It demonstrates to students that they are doing well.

9) Learning Objectives

It will not always be possible for students to have success criteria or a mark-scheme with which to assess their work. In fact, you may not always want them to have one of these options available. An alternative approach is for students to use their own knowledge of the subject and their previous learning. One possibility that always remains open though, is the use of the learning objective as something against which an assessment can be made.

Learning objectives have a number of purposes:

- To indicate to students what the lesson is about.
- To tell students what the lesson should help them to do.
- To help the teacher to plan.
- To minimise ambiguity.
- To tick boxes.

I include the last point because for some teachers that is what they feel like – something which has to be done to please someone else. It is worth noting that a good lesson is not dependent on its having a learning objective. Such a proposition is plainly absurd if subjected to any degree of analysis.

The first two points are important though, and I would wager that most teachers will agree that students will do better if they know what the lesson is about and what exactly it is intended to help them to do. The key point is that, while learning objectives provide a way to meet these aims, they are not the only way.

Personally, I think learning objectives are a quick and convenient method by which to convey to students what the lesson will be about and what it will help them to do. I also think that they can be used in a number of ways which are beneficial to teachers and to students. One of these works as follows:

Use your learning objective as the main criteria by which students are instructed to self-assess. Put aside five to ten minutes at the end of your lesson and ask students to think about whether or not they have met the learning objective and, if they have, what evidence they have to demonstrate this. Some methods you could use for this are:

- Students discuss in pairs whether they feel they have met the learning objective. They then write their thoughts up in their books.
- Students write a paragraph explaining to what extent they think they have met the learning objective. They provide evidence to support their claims. This will be in the form of examples taken from what they have done during the lesson.
- Students draw a line in their book and label the ends 'completely' and 'not at all'. The teacher asks the question: 'To what extent have you met the learning objective?' Students indicate their answers on their lines and then each write a paragraph explaining why this is the case. If necessary, they set themselves a target for improvement.

10) Using Pro-Forma

A pro-forma can be an excellent way of structuring student self-assessments. It can help scaffold such activities for pupils, making them easier to access and complete. In addition, they can be designed so as to encourage students to think in certain ways or to reflect on specific areas of their work. One example pro-forma, which you might like to use, works as follows:

Divide a sheet of A4-paper into thirds. In the top two thirds draw three boxes of equal size. In the bottom third, write the following questions:

1) What have you learnt this lesson?
2) What strengths can you identify in your work today?
3) What skills have you used today? Have you used them well?
4) What new knowledge have you learnt today? Give an example of how or when you might use it.

5) How might you improve what you have done today? Why would it be an improvement?
6) Based on today's lesson and the work you have produced, what could be your target for next lesson?
7) How might you have done things differently today? Why?
8) What is the best thing you have done in today's lesson and why?
9) What do you know now that you did not know at the start of the lesson?
10) How might we build on today's learning in the future?

Create enough sheets for your class and hand them out at the end of the lesson. Invite students to select three questions. They should write these in the three boxes and then set about answering them.

11) Learning Journal

Learning journals are a way for students to keep track of their self-assessments. They allow pupils and teachers to look at the progress which is being made over an extended period of time. They provide continuity and help students to develop their skills of reflection.

It is up to you how you construct the learning journal that your students will use. Here are some possible approaches:

- Provide each student with a blank exercise book. They label this with the title 'Learning Journal' and their name.
- Create a bespoke learning journal. You can use Microsoft PowerPoint or Microsoft Word to make a series of pages containing instructions and directions for students. Some of these could be highly structured pro-forma while others could be left relatively open.

- Spend a lesson creating a learning journal with your class. Explain what the purpose of the document will be and then divide students into groups. Give each group a different category and ask them to produce two pages for the learning journal. At the end of the lesson, collect in the pages that groups have produced. Photocopy these and create a booklet which is handed out to all students in the next lesson. Categories which you might give to the different groups include: reflection; strengths and targets; learning objectives; drawing; compare with a peer, and so on.
- Create a learning journal based on the layout of a diary.
- If you have computer access, ask your students to keep an online journal. This could be a Microsoft PowerPoint or a Microsoft Word document that you create and then share with your students. Another alternative is to ask pupils to keep a blog of their learning, although it will probably be best to keep this on your intranet (internal to the school) rather than to publish it on the internet (publicly accessible).

12) Skills and Knowledge Audit

A year is a long time. Often in school, as the days tumble past and one lesson stacks on top of another, we lose sight of just how much teaching teachers do and just how much learning pupils engage in.

What a student knows and can do at the beginning of a year is vastly different to what they know and can do at the end of a year. This is an obvious point. It is worth mentioning however because gradual change experienced up close is often difficult to observe. Last week I made a visit to a school in which I used to teach. In a short space of time some of the students in my old tutor group had changed significantly – both in terms of their physical appearances and their intellectual abilities. Of course, to my former colleagues, who had been there all along, this change was not as noticeable. Returning after an absence, my point of reference was quite different. This made the contrast stark and therefore all the more affecting.

A skills and knowledge audit allows you to create this experience for students. It works as follows:

At the beginning of the year, create a document which contains all the things which you will study with your class and all the skills that they will be expected to use and develop. Beside each item, leave five boxes for indicating confidence levels. These should state: not confident; a little confident; fairly confident; very confident; and super confident.

It may well be the case that your document runs to five or more pages. That is fine. It gives an indication of just how much you and your students will be doing over the course of the year.

At the start of the year, hand out the audit and ask students to write their names on it. They should then go through and indicate how they feel in relation to each of the skills or areas of knowledge, ticking the relevant boxes.

At various points in the year, ask pupils to take out their audits again and to use a different colour to indicate how they now feel about the various skills and areas of knowledge. Each juncture will provide you and your students with an opportunity to identify how much progress has been made, where confidence levels have improved the most, and any areas that need to be revisited. By the end of the year, it is likely that each student will have a document bedecked in different colours, clearly demonstrating just how much they have learnt. It will be akin to a record of progress for their time spent in your lessons (and could be used as a diagnostic tool by their next teacher).

Chapter Seven - Giving Feedback

Instead of giving students a mark or a grade, give three strengths and a target. The strengths should indicate good things the student has done and make it clear why these are deemed to be good things. The target should indicate one thing the student can do to improve their work. It should also explain why this will be an improvement and, if possible, include an example of what such an improvement will look like.

By giving three strengths you will be helping you students to accept your developmental comment. They will experience success and therefore feel motivated to take on board your target. Do not be tempted to give fewer strengths than this – keep the ratio high. Do not be tempted to give more targets – one thing is enough. When that has been mastered, then it will be time to move onto something else.

It is important that all your strengths and targets focus on the student's learning, or things which are closely connected to this. That way, you are coaching them on how to get better. In addition, by explaining why the strengths represent good things and why the target will lead to an improvement, you will be opening up the assessment criteria for students and making them aware of what it is they are being judged against (and, therefore, what it is they are being asked to do and to learn).

This chapter is divided into two sections:

    i.   Example strengths. I have provided two hundred examples of strengths you might give to students. These are divided into ten general categories. They are all generic – none are subject-specific. You can lift them straight out of the book and use them when marking, or you can use them as the basis for developing your own strengths.

ii.   Example targets. As above, except with targets instead of strengths.

The aim of the chapter is to make the process of giving formative feedback as easy as possible. The examples and lists will save you time and help you on your way.

Strengths:

Skills of Argument

Issues of Content

Gaining Mastery

Thinking Deeper

Speaking and Listening

Precision and Accuracy

Language and Vocabulary

Developing Creativity

Working with Others

Reading and Writing

Targets:

Skills of Argument

Issues of Content

Gaining Mastery

Thinking Deeper

Self-Assessment

Precision and Accuracy

Speaking and Listening

Language and Vocabulary

Developing Creativity

Skills of Analysis

Example Strengths

Skills of Argument

1. Excellent use of reasons. You have made it quite clear why you believe we should accept your argument to be true.

2. **You have used clear reasoning throughout. This means that you have stated why you think certain things are the case. It demonstrates that you have analysed them carefully.**

3. You have used evidence to support your arguments. Well done. This makes your points more convincing because it offers them support.

4. **Excellent selection of evidence. You have picked things which clearly connect to the reasons you have outlined. This makes your argument logical and persuasive.**

5. Good use of examples. You have thought carefully about how best to explain your points. This makes it easier for the reader to understand what you are trying to say.

6. **The examples you have used are thoughtful. They demonstrate your understanding of the topic and show that you can express this clearly through argument.**

7. You have expressed yourself clearly throughout. This means that your argument is easy to follow and accurately communicates your ideas to the reader.

8. **You have expressed your own ideas about the topic. Well done. This shows that you have been thinking carefully and paying attention in class.**

9. Your argument is clear and therefore easy to understand.

10. You have made your points clearly and put them in an order which helps the reader to see how they connect.

11. An excellent choice of structure for your argument. It creates a logical flow which makes your writing easy to understand and more persuasive.

12. By collecting your points together into two different sections you have created a well-structured argument.

13. You make good use of logic throughout your argument. It is clear how your points lead on to one another. This makes your argument more powerful.

14. You have employed an excellent logical structure. As a result, your various points fit together into a seamless whole.

15. Excellent use of linking sentences to create continuity in your argument. It is clear that you have thought carefully about how to take the reader from one point to the next.

16. Well done for linking your argument back to the question. This has helped to keep your work focussed throughout.

17. You have come up with a really original perspective. This makes your argument interesting and engaging, drawing in the reader.

18. You have developed a series of original points. This shows you have been thinking carefully about the topic and your own feelings towards it.

19. Your argument displays an admirable degree of balance. This makes the reader feel as if you are prepared to consider a variety of viewpoints before coming to a conclusion.

20. This is a really balanced argument. You have been sure to include points both for and against. This demonstrates a careful, critical engagement with the topic.

Issues of Content

1. Well done, your work displays excellent knowledge of what we have been studying.

2. **It is clear that you have developed a good knowledge of the key content. This is evident from the way in which you make use of it in your work.**

3. Excellent use of the key concepts in your work. It is clear from what you have produced that you understand these and know how to use them accurately.

4. **Your work demonstrates a good understanding of the key concepts in the topic. You have clearly demonstrated what they mean and provided examples as well.**

5. Your work shows a high degree of accuracy throughout. You have obviously been paying close attention to what we have been studying. Well done.

6. **Accurate use of the content we have been looking at. It is clear from your work that you have thought carefully about the material and that you understand exactly what it is and what it means.**

7. Throughout your work you use the keywords correctly. This demonstrates that you know what they mean and are confident in putting them into practice. Well done.

8. **You have taken great care to ensure that you are making accurate and precise use of the key content and concepts we have studied in lessons. Good work.**

9. There is a real range of content evident in your work. This breadth suggests that you have really got to grips with the topic and that you understand exactly what it encompasses.

10. By using a range of different ideas you have demonstrated your excellent, in-depth understanding of the topic. Well done.

11. In a number of places you have specified precisely what it is you mean or what you take a keyword to mean. This is good because it makes it clear that you are thinking carefully about the topic.

12. It is clear that you have taken great care in choosing which examples to use in your work. This demonstrates a good knowledge of the content – otherwise you would not be in a position to make such choices.

13. Your work shows a clear understanding of when it is appropriate to use the keywords.

14. Your work shows clearly that you understand how different parts of what we have studied connect together. This is good because it suggests you are thinking broadly about the topic.

15. There are a number of examples in your work where you have developed the ideas we have looked at in lessons in your own direction. This shows original thinking and a desire to make the ideas your own. Well done.

16. Well done for using what we have studied in lessons to develop an original piece of work. This demonstrates how you have understood the content and then taken it on to create something expressing your own ideas.

17. Excellent analysis of the key ideas we have been studying. You have broken them down and made it clear how they work and what goes to make them up.

18. You have made good use of your analytical skills to break the content down in order to explain it. This

demonstrates a sound understanding of what we have been studying.

19. Good application of the ideas we have been looking at in lessons. Your work shows that you know how these work and when it is appropriate to use them.

20. It is clear from your work that you understand how to use the key concepts we have been studying. I have indicated a number of points where your use of them is absolutely correct.

Gaining Mastery

1. There is clear evidence that you are able to skilfully manipulate the content in order to serve your purpose. This is excellent and demonstrates a growing mastery in your work.

2. **You have made thoughtful use of the material we have looked at in order to produce work of a very high standard. This suggests you are increasingly able to distinguish what it is that is useful given the demands of the task.**

3. I can see significant developments in your work over the past few months. You are increasingly able to express yourself fluently in the subject. Well done.

4. **Over time you have demonstrated an increasing ability to use the key ideas we have looked at in lessons with skill and accuracy. Your most recent work is the best example of this yet. Well done.**

5. Your work shows the benefits of practice. Evidently you have been working at developing your skills and I am pleased to say that this has paid off. Keep it up.

6. **This work shows me that you have been practising in order to improve. The result is that you are expressing yourself more clearly and are showing a better understanding of what we have been studying.**

7. Well done for assessing your own work and identifying how you might improve it. The target you have set is thoughtful and shows me that you know what you need to do to get better in the subject.

8. **I am delighted to see that you assessed your work when you finished it and then improved it as a result. This**

shows that you are taking control of your learning and being independent.

9. Your latest work shows a much more accurate use of the key vocabulary we have been learning.

10. **There are major improvements in your writing. You have developed your work so that you express your ideas more clearly.**

11. It is clear that you have developed an excellent understanding of the key ideas we have been studying. Your work shows that you comprehend them and have found ways of putting them to use.

12. **Excellent exploration of the key ideas we have been considering this term. It is evident from what you have produced that you have developed a real mastery of these, including an understanding of how they might be used.**

13. Your work shows you to be in control of the content we have been studying recently. You are able to use it with increasing skill and accuracy.

14. **Comparing your current work to what you produced earlier in the term, it is clear to see that you have developed your understanding of the topic quite considerably. Well done.**

15. In a short space of time you have gotten to grips with the new ideas we have been studying and are now using them confidently in your work.

16. **Since beginning the topic it is clear that you have worked hard to develop your understanding. The results of this can be seen in your most recent work, which is of a very high standard indeed.**

17. Your writing increasingly reflects that of a historian (insert other term as appropriate). You are using the conventions of the subject and thinking carefully about how one who is studying the discipline ought to write.

18. **The contributions you make in class reflect an increasing understanding of what the subject is about.**

19. Your work shows an increasing proficiency. This is evident from the decrease in the number of errors and the increase in consistency across the various things you have done in class and at home. Well done.

20. **I can see from the way in which you are answering questions that your confidence in the subject is developing. This is a result of the hard work you are putting in. Keep it up.**

Thinking Deeper

1. It is clear that you have developed a sound grasp of the key concepts we have been studying.

2. **Your work shows a sound understanding of the concepts which are central to the subject. The result of this is that you are expressing your ideas skilfully.**

3. I can see that you are taking the time to explore the ideas we have been considering in depth. This is good because it shows a clear engagement with the subject and will also help you to further develop your understanding.

4. **It is a feature of your work that you explore what ideas mean and how they might affect people and the world around us. Well done.**

5. You consistently make unusual connections between different ideas, concepts and examples. This is excellent as it shows you are thinking carefully about the work and are considering how it might relate to other areas of your learning.

6. **There are many occasions (I have highlighted some) where you connect ideas or examples together in original ways. This shows creative thinking which is closely engaged with what we are doing in class.**

7. You frequently connect elements of what we are studying to your own experience. This helps to contextualise your learning and shows that you are connecting it to what else you know.

8. **Your use of personal experience to supplement the ideas and content we are looking at in lessons is excellent. It really brings home the real-world relevance of what we are studying.**

9. I have indicated a number of points where you have made connections with other areas of the curriculum. This is really good. It shows that you understand the work we do in class is not isolated, but is in fact connected to other areas of learning.

10. **Excellent use of current events to exemplify the concepts and ideas we have been looking at in lesson.**

11. Your answers display a great deal of thought and careful consideration. For example, this last piece of work considers a range of viewpoints, many of which would not have been immediately apparent.

12. **I am pleased to see how much thought you are putting into your work. It is clear that you are engaging carefully with what we are doing in lessons.**

13. This is an excellent piece of analysis. You provide a detailed breakdown of the material, showing what makes it up and how the separate parts fit together.

14. **Your work demonstrates sound analysis throughout. You have investigated the topic carefully. Little, if anything, escapes your attention.**

15. It is clear from the extent of your evaluation that you have a sound understanding of the content. You highlight a variety of strengths and weaknesses, remaining critical throughout.

16. **You have engaged critically with the material, considering it in light of what you understand about the topic and the subject. This has resulted in work which is highly evaluative.**

17. Much of what you have done has been highly original and creative. This is good because it shows that you are

prepared to take the material on and develop it in ways which you think are best.

18. **Your work shows great originality. This stems from your knowledge of the subject and your confidence in developing your own thoughts and perspectives. Well done.**

19. You are working hard in lessons and completing all the extension tasks. This is really good to see. Keep it up, as its helping to develop your thinking.

20. **The answers you are giving to the extension tasks demonstrate an ability to think deeply about the subject.**

Speaking and Listening

1. You are expressing your own point of view clearly and confidently. This is good because it is helping you to articulate and further develop your thoughts. It also means that others can hear your ideas.

2. **In class discussions you frequently put forward your own ideas. This helps others to learn and also allows you to find out what others think about your ideas.**

3. There have been many times over the last term where you have made really thoughtful contributions to class discussions and debates. Well done.

4. **On many occasions the contributions you have made in class have moved the learning on and helped everybody to better understand the topic. Keep it up.**

5. When you speak in class you exhibit a calm confidence. This is clearly a result of your sound understanding of the material we are studying which, in turn, is down to your hard work and application.

6. **You are not afraid to speak out in class or to put forward an opinion which differs from what others think. This shows independence and strength of character – two great traits to keep developing.**

7. It is noticeable that you think before you speak in class discussions. The result of this is that what you say is clear, logical and thoughtful.

8. **Your discussion contributions demonstrate that you think carefully about how to express yourself. This is good because it means your comments communicate accurately what it is that you are thinking.**

9. Through a combination of confident speaking and thoughtful reasoning you are able to argue persuasively in class discussions and debates.

10. **When you speak in class you often put forward persuasive arguments. These are based on a careful use of language and the marshalling of credible and convincing reasons, evidence and examples.**

11. I have noticed that during discussions and debates you listen carefully to whoever is talking. This demonstrates a real respect for the speaker and is also a powerful way of developing your own understanding.

12. **You frequently model excellent listening. This involves looking at the speaker, paying attention and responding, if appropriate, to what it is they are saying. Well done.**

13. The comments you make in discussions demonstrate that you have listened carefully to what has been said. This is because they tend to link directly to what has already been talked about.

14. **When you are part of a discussion, it is clear from your comments that you are taking on board that which other people are saying.**

15. Throughout the term you have asked really thoughtful questions about the work we have been doing. This suggests that you are listening carefully to what is said in class and then analysing the material as well.

16. **There have been a number of occasions where you have asked other students to explain their points, to give examples or to clarify what they are saying. This is excellent. It demonstrates that you are listening carefully and then thinking critically about what is being said.**

17. Well done for maintaining an open mind during our discussions. I have seen you develop and alter your opinions a number of times, based on what you have heard. This shows that you are prepared to listen to different ideas.

18. **You show considerable patience when waiting to speak during discussions. This is good because it shows respect and also suggests that you are listening to others even though there is something you would like to share.**

19. It has been clear throughout the term how you have been supportive of others during group, paired and whole-class discussion. Well done, you are helping them to learn and displaying admirable conduct at the same time.

20. **Excellent adaptation of your language and presentation style in order to meet the demands of the audience.**

Precision and Accuracy

1. You are expressing yourself clearly in your work. It is clear what you think and what reasons you have for thinking this.

2. **Your work demonstrates a high level of clarity. This suggests that you are accurately expressing yourself.**

3. I have highlighted a series of instances where you have used key terms correctly. This shows you are really getting to grips with the language linked to this topic.

4. **There is clear evidence that you are able to use key terminology accurately. This shows a good understanding of the topic.**

5. From the contributions you are making in class it is evident that you have an accurate understanding of the topic.

6. **The understanding of the topic demonstrated throughout your work is consistently accurate. This stems from your knowledge of the key ideas we have looked at in lessons. Well done.**

7. You have continually answered the question in your work, never once deviating. This is excellent. The accuracy of response means you are doing exactly what has been asked of you.

8. **In every answer you keep linking your points back to the question. This ensures that your answer remains precisely focussed on the demands of the question.**

9. Your work in class and at home shows that you are paying close attention to what the tasks ask you to do. As a result, you are producing material of a consistently high standard.

10. I am impressed at how you have analysed the requirements of the task and then used these to inform your work. The result is a high level of precision in relation to what has been asked of you.

11. It is pleasing to see how you have made use of the assessment criteria to plan and execute your work. This has resulted in material of a high standard.

12. **You have made accurate use of the success criteria in the planning of your work. This has led to material which addresses all the key points necessary to receive high marks.**

13. There is evidence of you taking great care over your work. It shows significant attention to detail.

14. **Your work shows a high level of attention to detail. This has led you to create responses which are accurate and precise, showing a careful consideration of what it is that the tasks require.**

15. I note that you have refined your work in a number of places. This is good as it shows you are paying attention to how you might improve.

16. **I am pleased to see that you have refined your work. This suggests that you are looking critically at what you have done, comparing it the question or task and then making improvements.**

17. Throughout your work you have chosen appropriate examples and evidence which accurately support the arguments you have made.

18. **Your choice of structure for this work was exactly right. It has allowed you to meet the demands of the task and to demonstrate a high level of skill at the same time.**

19. Your use of self-assessment to check the accuracy and precision of your work is first rate. Keep it up.

20. **It is evident that you have developed your work through the use of self-assessment. I can see evidence of where you have improved the accuracy of things you have revisited.**

Language and Vocabulary

1. Excellent use of the keywords we have been studying. Your work shows that you understand their meaning and how to use them in a sentence.

2. **It is clear that you have developed a good understanding of the keywords in the subject. I have indicated where you have used them correctly – which is in the majority of your work.**

3. You have made skilled use of technical vocabulary. This is good because it raises the level of your work, making it more formal and more suited to the subject.

4. **There is some excellent application of technical vocabulary in your work. It is clear that you understand what these terms mean and when they should be used.**

5. Throughout your writing there is evidence that you understand the language of the subject and that you know how to use it correctly. Well done.

6. **Thoughtful choice of keywords. This indicates a clear understanding of their correct usage.**

7. I have indicated a number of occasions where your choice of language demonstrates particularly careful thought. You have chosen the right words to convey your meaning.

8. **It is evident from your work that you are thinking carefully about what language to use and when to use it.**

9. Your work shows an extensive vocabulary being put to good use. It makes your writing engaging, persuasive and enjoyable to read.

10. I am impressed by the range of words you have used and have indicated occasions I think to be particularly worthy of note.

11. You are writing more academically, which is excellent. It makes your work feel more formal and less like a conversation. Well done.

12. I can see that you are really focussing on developing your style so that it is more academic. You have definitely succeeded in doing this. Your writing is more and more appropriate to the tasks we are doing.

13. Your work is becoming like that of a historian/scientist/mathematician. You are weaving the conventions of the discipline into your writing. Keep it up.

14. It is clear that you understand how a historian/scientist/mathematician ought to write. I can see that you are applying the conventions of the discipline to your work.

15. This is an excellent piece of work. You have really understood the genre and have used many of the conventions and techniques which go with it.

16. I am pleased to see that you have made use of the appropriate dramatic elements in your work, as we discussed. This has made your writing feel much more as if it is of the genre.

17. You have achieved a great deal of clarity through your use of language. Your meaning is communicated simply and clearly. Well done.

18. I can see that you have thought carefully about what language to use. This is because your choice of words

puts across very precisely what it is that you are trying to say.

19. Your work contains accurate spelling and punctuation throughout. This means that it communicates more clearly to the reader. It also demonstrates a high level of understanding.

20. **You have made use of logical sentence and paragraph structures throughout your work. This helps to ensure your writing is clear and easy to read.**

Developing Creativity

1. Your work contains a number of original ideas. I am impressed by this creative thinking. It shows that you are pushing yourself to develop the ideas we are studying.

2. **Excellent, original ideas throughout your work. These demonstrate how carefully you are thinking about the topic.**

3. You have made some unusual connections in your work. This is good as it shows that you are looking to develop your thinking on the topic.

4. **I have indicated some of the unusual connections which you have made. I like these and am impressed by the originality of your thinking. Well done.**

5. In recent weeks you have really jumped into the tasks in lesson and made them your own. This has led you to produce creative and original work.

6. **The way you have put your own spin on this task is great. It demonstrates a real independence of mind as well as some thoughtful, creative thinking.**

7. Your work is innovative. It goes beyond what is the norm and takes the ideas we have been looking at in new and creative directions.

8. **I am impressed at how you have innovated in class in recent weeks. Your ideas and suggestions have really helped your group to create some fantastically original work.**

9. The way in which you have responded to the task shows that you have thought carefully about how you can best convey your ideas. The results are creative and original.

10. **There is clear evidence that you have created your own individual style of response to the analysis tasks we have been practising recently. Well done.**

11. A feature of your work is that you make thoughtful connections to other subjects and areas of the curriculum. This creative thinking situates the ideas we have been studying in a broader context.

12. **I like the way in which you develop connections between what we are studying and other areas of the curriculum. Your use of similes is particularly creative.**

13. You have used the task as an opportunity to explore the idea in depth and to try to establish what it might mean in different contexts.

14. **Your exploration of the ideas shows a creative approach to analysis. This is particularly evident from the way in which you have used unusual examples to support your points.**

15. The examples you have called on in your work indicate a creative approach to the task. They are far from standard and cause the reader to think differently about what is a familiar topic.

16. **You have clearly taken time to develop examples to support your points. The result is a creative piece of work which is original rather than repetitive. Well done.**

17. I am impressed at how you have taken risks in your answers. This has resulted in some particularly creative responses which shed new light on the ideas we have been studying.

18. It was a risk to approach the work in this way but the results have been really good. You have created an unusual and original response to the topic.

19. I have been pleased to see you trying out different possibilities in your group and paired work in class. This has allowed you to explore different areas of the learning.

20. Your work shows a thoughtful consideration of the different possibilities that could stem from what we have been studying.

Working with Others

1. It is evident from your work in class that you are supportive of those people around you. This is excellent as it demonstrates a concern for others as well as an understanding of how to help them.

2. **You have continually supported the members of the class with who you have been working. This is a strong attribute to have and one you should keep using.**

3. Your work in groups this term has helped other members of the class to learn. This is to your great credit.

4. **The contributions you make in class help others to learn by giving them an insight into your thinking. Keep it up.**

5. You have displayed great leadership skills in class. You are prepared to step forward and take charge of tasks and to help others to achieve their best.

6. **There have been a number of occasions where you have led the learning in class. This has come when we have worked in groups, as well as when we have been in whole-class discussion.**

7. You have displayed a real talent for collaborating with others. This has been evident from the work you have helped to create when part of a group.

8. **It is clear that you understand what is necessary for successful collaboration. You have helped the groups in which you have been a member to create some excellent pieces of work throughout the term.**

9. When you are engaged in group work it is clear that you listen carefully to the thoughts of others. This demonstrates a great deal of respect and is an important prerequisite for successful analysis.

10. **Your listening skills when working with others are excellent. I have noted a number of occasions where you have helped your group to understand one another's points by listening carefully and then explaining the various views which have been aired.**

11. It is clear from your writing that you give due consideration to other people's views. This is good because it creates more balanced work.

12. **There are a number of points where it is clear you have taken on board what other people have said. This is good because it shows you are thinking carefully about your own arguments and how to develop them.**

13. You are not afraid to put forward your views and to hold your ground if others do not agree with you. This is an excellent ability to have as it shows independence and confidence.

14. **I have noted a number of occasions where you have put forward views which others in the class do not share. It is excellent that you are prepared to stand up for your beliefs and try to persuade others that they are right.**

15. You take time in lessons to keep others on track and focussed. This comes from your positive attitude towards learning and your desire to help others. Well done.

16. **When those around you lose focus you are quick to pull them back on track. This is of great benefit to their learning and reflects well on your own character.**

17. You exert a positive influence on students with who you work. This stems from your desire to do well and to engage positively with the learning.

18. **When working in groups you act as a positive influence on your peers, directing them toward the learning and the task in hand.**

19. I have been pleased to see you guiding other learners in how to go about the work. It is to your credit that you are using your knowledge and understanding to help other people to learn.

20. **I have been delighted with your support as a leader of learning/student teacher/expert helper this term. Well done for using your grasp of the subject to help others.**

Reading and Writing

1. It is clear from your work that you have fully understood the meaning of the text. You have made relevant explanations in a manner which is clear and precise.

2. **Your answers suggest that you have read the text carefully and understand what the author is trying to say.**

3. You have made good use of the information we have been looking at. This is clear from how you have applied it to your own arguments.

4. **I can see from your answers that you understand the information. You have applied your knowledge with skill and flair.**

5. Your work contains some excellent analysis. You have broken the text down and pulled it apart in order to explain how it works.

6. **There is clear evidence here of thoughtful analysis. Your writing explicitly details the various elements which influence the ideas we have been studying.**

7. Excellent evaluation. You have presented a range of arguments both for and against, before coming to a conclusion.

8. **Your writing shows a careful consideration of the various points, coupled with a considered judgement about which is most persuasive.**

9. I am impressed at how you have incorporated the material we have looked at into your own work. This suggests you are thinking creatively about how to make use of it.

10. **Well done. You have successfully brought a number of different elements into your work, giving it a sense of purpose and direction.**

11. From your answers I can see that you have understood the texts we have been studying. It is clear that you are able to apply yourself to analysis with skill and precision.

12. **There is clear evidence in your work of a developed understanding of what the text is saying.**

13. I am pleased at how you are developing your answers. You frequently make extra points and give detailed examples to help flesh out your work.

14. **On a number of occasions you have developed your answers in greater detail. This is excellent because it demonstrates that you are thinking carefully about the topic and how best to display your knowledge and understanding.**

15. The level of detail in your writing is superb. No stone is left unturned as you seek to explore the ideas and information in great depth.

16. **The extent of your analysis is impressive. The level of detail with which you explain the key issues suggests that you have an excellent understanding of what they are and how they are structured.**

17. Throughout your work you use a variety of evidence and a range of examples. This is good because it shows that you are thinking broadly about the topic.

18. **There is a nice range of evidence and examples in your work. This suggests to the reader that you understand the topic in depth.**

19. It is clear from your work that you have been able to unlock the meaning in the text. You note various levels and the interactions between these.

20. **I can see from your work that you are able to pick apart the text so as to draw out the variety of meanings which it holds. Well done – this is high-level analysis.**

Example Targets

Skills of Argument

1. Always give reasons to support any claims you make. Reasons use logic to demonstrate why what you say is correct. For example: 'Ice cream is the best...**because it is sweet as well as cool.**'

2. **Give examples to support the arguments you make. Examples give the audience a real-life situation or case which demonstrates the truth of what you are saying.**

3. Give evidence to support the arguments you make. Evidence means something in the real-world which supports your argument. For example: 'The X-Factor is popular. Evidence to support this includes viewing figures of more than ten million.'

4. **Try using counter-arguments in your writing. A counter-argument goes against the main argument. By showing why the counter-argument is wrong, you strengthen your own case.**

5. Give multiple reasons to support the claims you make. By giving more than one reason, you will make your argument more persuasive.

6. **Ensure your argument follows a logical path. Each point should link clearly to the previous one and to the overall argument.**

7. Connect together the different reasons you use. Showing how reasons link can make your argument more persuasive.

8. **Consider different viewpoints in your writing. Try to show how different people may make different arguments about the same issue.**

9. Contrast different viewpoints in your writing. Show how they may be similar and/or different, and explain why this might be the case.

10. **Plan in advance the overall structure of your argument. Group together similar points and themes. Only move on when you have written all you wish to write about a particular area.**

11. Ensure your introduction is clear and to the point. It should address the question and indicate what you will be writing about.

12. **Ensure your conclusion is brief and relevant. It should be a short, evaluative summary which touches on the points you have made without introducing any new material.**

13. When writing an extended argument, try to use a 'for and against' structure. Look first at why people might argue in favour of the proposition and then look at why they might argue against it. This structure promotes clarity.

14. **Ensure the conclusions you draw come directly from the reasons you give. If you have a conclusion which does not relate to your reasons (or evidence), it is not a valid conclusion. For example: If A, then B. If B then C. Therefore, if A then C. This is a valid conclusion, because it stems directly from the preceding reasons.**

15. Ensure you answer the question throughout. Every paragraph should explicitly answer the question.

16. **Before you begin, consider what the main focus of your argument is. This will ensure you think carefully about the position you are putting forward.**

17. Write to persuade. Remember, you need to **convince** people of the truth of your argument. They may not necessarily agree with you.

18. **Before you begin, consider all the points you wish to make. Put them in the order which you feel is most persuasive. Stick to this plan as you write your answer.**

19. Plan your answer in advance. Think about what your argument is, the different points you will make, and the order in which you will make them. Doing this will increase the clarity and persuasiveness of your writing.

20. **Evaluate the arguments you make. This means pointing out the strengths and weaknesses of the arguments. By doing this, you will demonstrate your understanding of the validity of the arguments.**

1. Increase the level of detail in your work. Including more information and ideas will help you to think more carefully about the topic.

2. **When answering questions or completing tasks, ensure you are accurate in your use of language. Practise using subject-specific language correctly. Use a glossary, dictionary or thesaurus to help.**

3. When answering questions or completing tasks, ensure you are precise. If you are being asked about a certain area of the topic, stick to that area in your answer.

4. **Use evidence to demonstrate what it is you are saying or writing. For example: if you make a claim about the topic, give evidence to support that claim.**

5. Ensure your work consistently connects to the topic. You should be able to connect everything you mention to the topic we are focussing on.

6. **Practise using the keywords, ideas and concepts we look at. Make sure you are familiar with their definitions. This will help you to use them correctly.**

7. Go back over what we have been studying and revise the content. Create flashcards to help you. Do this until you are more confident in your understanding of the material.

8. **Work with a friend or a family member. Ask them to test your knowledge of what we are studying. Go over any material you are struggling with until you are successful every time.**

9. Ensure you consistently evaluate the information we look at. Highlight its strengths and weaknesses, as well as the effects it might have on individuals and the world.

10. **Ensure you consistently analyse the content we look at. This means you break the content down and examine the different aspects of it, as well as how these connect to one another.**

11. When you have finished a piece of work, go back through it and check your use of keywords, ideas and information. Ask yourself whether you have used these correctly – check with a partner, dictionary or textbook if you can.

12. **Practise using the knowledge you get in lessons in everyday life. Search for opportunities to do this at home, in school, or when you are out and about.**

13. Learn the definitions of keywords and key concepts off by heart. Ask a friend or a family member to test you. Or, write the word on one side of a card and the definition on another. You can use these to test yourself.

14. **From lesson to lesson, try to identify the similarities and differences between topic areas. Include these comparisons in your answers. It will demonstrate a broad understanding of the subject.**

15. Consider the relationships between different concepts we study. Try to demonstrate some of these connections in your work. Show how these different concepts influence or affect one another.

16. **Before you start writing, think carefully about the purpose of the writing and who the audience is. Select your content accordingly. Different purposes and different audiences may well demand different content.**

17. Create a glossary at the back of your book. Every time you come across a new word, write it down, along with its definition, in your glossary.

18. **Every time you encounter a new word, aim to use it three times in the next couple of lessons. This will help you to get familiar with the meaning of the word and the contexts in which it can be used.**

19. When you finish a piece of work, swap books with a partner. Go through and assess whether they have used subject-specific language correctly. If they have not, give examples of how they can improve.

20. **Try to make connections between the content we look at in our lessons, and what you do in other subjects. Where possible, draw out these connections in your work.**

Gaining Mastery

1. When you have finished a piece of work, go through it and identify how you can improve it. Redo the work taking account of the improvements. Then, if you have time, repeat the process to further refine your work.

2. **Choose an aspect of the subject which you find difficult. Practise this aspect regularly, both in and out of lessons. Look for opportunities to engage with the aspect. Doing so repeatedly will help you to come to terms with it.**

3. Repeat **skill X** over and over. Each time, scrutinise what you do. Find ways you can improve with each repetition.

4. **Repeat question/task type X over and over. Each time, examine how your response is related to the question/task. Through this process, you will come to understand the demands of the question/task more clearly.**

5. Every lesson, reflect on what it is you have learnt and the way you have learnt it. Keep a diary of your thoughts. Use these to analyse how you are learning and, in turn, how you can maximise your learning.

6. **Take time to reflect on how the work you produce relates to the learning you do in lessons. Critically examine the relationship between the two: analyse how one leads to the other. By understanding this, you will be in a better position to direct your own learning on the subject.**

7. Reflect on how you are using the learning you do in lessons. Are you thinking carefully about it? Are you giving consideration to how, when and why it ought to be used? Are you aware of how your work is (or is not) exhibiting that learning?

8. When you finish a piece of work, look back over it and highlight where you have used new learning from the lesson. After you have done this, identify how you might develop that use in the future.

9. How might our learning concerning the topic be influenced or altered by the context in which we put it to use? In your future work, consider the influence of context on the skills you are using.

10. Try to demonstrate how the concepts and ideas we look at can have different meanings or uses depending on context. Develop your ideas through your future work.

11. Develop your understanding of the ideas we are studying by comparing and contrasting their use and meaning within different contexts. Make these contrasts explicit in your work.

12. Test the ideas we study by pushing them into different or unlikely contexts and seeing whether their meanings still hold. Make these experiments explicit in your work (including appropriate explanations).

13. Compare your own work concerning the ideas and information we are studying with 'model examples', for instance those in textbooks on the subject. Analyse how they differ and identify what you can do to get closer to the 'model examples'.

14. Find 'model examples' of individuals using the ideas which are central to our subject (for example, in textbooks, books or journals). Take copies of these and use them as a standard to aim for in your own work.

15. When you complete a piece of work, go back over it and identify two or three ways it could be improved. Instead of making the improvements, write out a rationale of why

the improvements would be a good thing. This will help you think actively about what success in the subject requires.

16. **When you complete a piece of work, go back over it and identify all the new ideas or information you have used. Critique your usage. Identify what you have done well and how you can improve your use of the ideas and information.**

17. Identify what the success criteria are in our subject. Namely, that which your work is being judged against. Once you have identified these, use them to plan your work.

18. **Use what you know about the subject, along with the evidence of your previous targets, and the strengths which have been pointed out about your work, to identify what it is that the subject requires. Once you have picked these out, work towards them.**

19. Search for examples of expert use of the concepts we are studying (for example: in textbooks, journals or on educational television programmes). Keep these close at hand and try to mimic them when using the same concepts.

20. **When you finish a piece of work, go through it and try to identify a series of minor adjustments you could make which would lead to an overall improvement. Repeat this process three or four times for each piece of work.**

Thinking Deeper

1. What do you think your target should be and why?

2. **How can you develop your work beyond what you are doing at present? Why will this be an improvement?**

3. Our next topic is **X**. Find out what has been written about it and be ready to talk and write about this in future lessons.

4. **Pick out all the subject-specific concepts you have used in your work so far. Explain whether you think you have used them correctly or not.**

5. Create an exam question based on our topic. Then, write a model answer.

6. **How might you use what we have learnt in other subjects/the future/your life?**

7. Before you begin your work, write down what you expect to communicate. Use this as a guide and, when you have finished, as a means to assess what you have done.

8. **Consider a range of viewpoints in your work. Put yourself in the shoes of other people and examine how their perspectives may be similar or different to your own.**

9. Evaluate the arguments you make. Identify their strengths and weaknesses. For example, 'A key strength of this argument is...'

10. **Aim to develop a critical mind-set in relation to the subject. Approach ideas with the attitude: 'How accurate is this? What is the evidence for it? How does it relate to what I already know?'**

11. Ensure your work progresses logically from start to finish, however long it is. The connections between each part of your work should be clear and coherent.

12. **Use a dictionary and thesaurus to ensure you are using language accurately. Check the meaning of words and whether or not you are employing them in the correct context.**

13. Make connections between the ideas we look at in lessons and the real world. This could include, for example, current news stories, or the jobs people do in society.

14. **Where possible, break questions down into separate parts and deal with each thing they ask in turn.**

15. Identify the command words in a question (these are the words which ask you to do something: discuss, examine, contrast and so on) and ensure your answer continually does what these words require.

16. **Problematize the concepts we look at. Demonstrate through your work how their meaning can be contested. For example: 'freedom' means different things to different people for different reasons.**

17. On finishing your work, write a rationale explaining why you have answered as you have. Detail the choices you have made and why you have made them. If this leads you to rewrite some of your work, that is OK.

18. **When you finish your work, write an extension question based on the topic. Then, answer the question.**

19. Compare and contrast different concepts with which we deal. Identify the relationships between the concepts and whether they are compatible or in conflict.

20. When finished, come up with two or three questions about the topic to which you would like to know the answers. For homework, research the answers.

Self-Assessment

1. When you finish, go back over your work and assess whether you have met the learning objectives or not. If you have, explain how. If you have not, improve it.

2. **When you finish, go back over your work and check it using SPS (Spelling; Punctuation; does it make Sense?). Make any improvements you think necessary.**

3. On finishing, identify the areas of the topic you feel most confident with and those you feel you need to do more work on. Make a note of these and follow up on them at the next opportunity.

4. **On finishing, make a list of questions you still want answered. Aim to find the answers either at home or in the next lesson.**

5. Having completed your work, compare it to the last piece of work you did which was similar. Identify how you have improved and what you could aim for next.

6. **Having completed your work, compare it to previous work you have done. Try to identify common mistakes you are making and target these as an area for improvement.**

7. When you have finished, look back over your work and identify three things you have done well and one thing you could improve. Follow up on this target in your next piece of work.

8. **On completing a piece of writing, read it aloud. Ask yourself whether it makes sense; if you have communicated clearly; and whether you could have said the same thing in fewer words. Make any changes you need to make.**

9. When you have finished, take two different coloured pens. Use one to highlight what you have done well and one to highlight a single thing you could improve.

10. **On completing a piece of work, read it through critically. This means you should actively look for ways in which it could be improved. Once you have done this, redraft the work so that it is better.**

11. When you finish, look back through your work and identify all the keywords you have used. Check to ensure you have used them accurately. If you have not, change your work. If you have used them correctly, choose two or three and explain how you know this to be the case.

12. **When you finish, write yourself an exam-style question based on the topic, along with a mark-scheme. Answer your question and then mark your work.**

13. On finishing, make a list of all the new information you have learnt in the lesson and all the skills you have practised. Put these in what you believe to be their order of importance.

14. **On finishing, identify all the concepts you have included in your work. Draw a map showing how these concepts link together. Then, identify whether you could have explained more of these links in your work.**

15. When you complete your work, shut your book. Imagine you are a person who knows nothing about the topic. Open your book and read through what you have written. Ask yourself how clear your answers are and how you could make them clearer.

16. **Having completed your work, set yourself a target for next lesson. The target should be something which will**

improve your work and which is focussed on your learning.

17. When you have finished, think back through the lesson and identify the different skills you have used. Note these down and comment on how effectively you have used them. Choose one to focus on, and try to improve, next lesson.

18. **When you have finished, go back through your work word-by-word. Aim to pick up on any mistake you have made, however small. Fix each one you encounter, only moving on when this is done.**

19. On completing a piece of work, take three different coloured highlighters and indicate which parts you feel are best, which are OK, and which could be improved (or, which you feel you need help with). Focus on the last two each time. Aim to get all your work up to the 'best' standard over the course of the term.

20. **Create a personal checklist of five things you think you need to improve. Use this checklist to assess every piece of work you do. Once you are consistently doing all the things on the checklist, write out a new one.**

Precision and Accuracy

1. Ensure you specify exactly what it is you mean. Avoid generalisations or talking vaguely about a topic. Be specific. Give examples which show precisely what you are trying to say.

2. **Tailor your answers to what a question or task is asking. Avoid straying into other areas or going off-topic. Remember: better communication is more precise.**

3. When you have finished a piece of work, analyse how accurately you have used keywords and ideas from our subject. Use definitions, examples and source material, such as textbooks, to help you.

4. **Try to consider how the context in which you are using concepts may influence their meaning. Concepts tend to vary in meaning depending on where, when and for what purpose they are being used.**

5. On completing your work, look back over it and analyse whether you are being consistent in your use of ideas. Is there variation between sentences, paragraphs and the overall piece? If so, try to correct this.

6. **Before beginning a paragraph, consider what points you will make, how they will connect, and how they ought to be ordered. This will help ensure you communicate your meaning more accurately.**

7. Practise using the key concepts and ideas we are looking at in lessons. This includes writing about them, talking about them and, where possible, doing them. Doing this will help you to use them with greater precision.

8. **Before you start a piece of work, consider what key ideas are going to be important. Having done this, analyse**

whether they are the correct ideas for this piece of work. If you are happy that they are, use them. If not, change them.

9. Aim for clarity. Clarity involves simplicity, precision and clearness. Go over any work you complete. Ask yourself: Is it easy to understand? Is it precise? Is it clear? If not, make the necessary changes.

10. **When you have completed a piece of extended written work, rewrite it so that the same meaning is conveyed through fewer words. This will make your work clearer and more precise.**

11. Aim for your work to have an overall coherency. Sentences should connect; paragraphs should link; the associations possessed by the things you write about should be made clear.

12. **Whenever you complete a piece of work, read it aloud. As you do this, consider these questions: Do the individual parts make sense? Do the individual parts connect in a meaningful way? Have I made myself clear? If you answer no to any of these questions, go back and improve your work.**

13. Remember that writing, speaking and doing all grow from what you are thinking. Look at the work you produce and consider whether they are as close as you can get to what is going on in your head. If they are not, work out how you can close the gap.

14. **When you complete a piece of work, ask a partner to read it aloud to you. While they are reading, analyse how accurately it reflects what you were trying to say. Then, make any changes you feel are necessary.**

15. Make regular use of a dictionary; have one nearby while you are working. Do not assume that your understanding of words is totally reliable. Use the dictionary to check. Doing so will improve your understanding.

16. **Before you begin your work identify: i) Who the audience is; ii) What the purpose of the work is; iii) What the success criteria are. This will help you to select the most appropriate language and style for your task.**

17. Think carefully about the skills you are using in lessons. Pick out examples of where you have done well and compare these to the times you have struggled. Use your findings to help you make improvements in the future.

18. **Identify the skills, relevant to the subject, you are best at. Having done this, analyse why you are good at them. Use this information to help tailor your future work and learning toward your strengths.**

19. Familiarise yourself with the success criteria/mark-scheme for our subject. Then, apply your knowledge to your work.

20. **On completing a piece of work, compare it to the success criteria/mark-scheme. Analyse how close your work is to that which is deemed ideal.**

Speaking and Listening

1. Before speaking, rehearse what you are going to say. You can do this in your mind or quietly, under your breath. This will improve the clarity of your speech, ensuring you pay close attention to your choice of words.

2. **Consider the pace at which you speak. Ensure you talk slowly enough for others to understand you, but fast enough to keep them engaged. This is called finding the right tempo.**

3. Before you speak, consider your audience. Different audiences require different styles of speech and different ways of speaking. For example: you talk differently when you are with your friends compared to when you are with your parents.

4. **When speaking, choose your words carefully. The quality of your language is vitally important to your being understood. Do not use unnecessary, inappropriate or over-the-top words or phrases.**

5. Aim for brevity when speaking. This does not mean your speech should be as short as possible. Rather, it means choosing the right words and the right length for the situation you are in.

6. **Before you speak, consider the purpose of your speech. Is it to persuade? Is it to clarify? Is it to share? Knowing why you are speaking allows you to tailor your speech accordingly.**

7. Avoid using para-language. This means words such as 'erm', 'ah', 'like', and so on. Speaking in this way diminishes the impact of what you are saying and can be off-putting for the audience.

8. **Use your body and face to supplement your speech. This can include making gestures, standing or sitting in a confident manner, and making eye contact.**

9. Practise using different rhetorical techniques in order to make your speech more persuasive. Examples include: asking rhetorical questions, speaking in threes, and leaving dramatic pauses.

10. **Aim to make at least one oral contribution per lesson. Speaking aloud is an important skill which enables you to share your ideas with others. It helps people to understand what you are thinking and it also help you to develop your own thoughts.**

11. Ensure you listen actively when others are speaking. This means concentrating on what they are saying. Make certain you are listening to the words they say and that you are thinking about the meaning of these.

12. **If you are uncertain about what someone is trying to say, ask them a clarifying question. For example: 'What exactly do you mean by that?' or, 'Could you explain that in more detail, please?'**

13. Ensure your body language shows that you are listening. Turn to face the speaker, look at them, and sit (or stand) respectfully. Remember, the speaker wants to 'see' that you are listening.

14. **Identify areas of ambiguity or vagueness in a speaker's words. When they have finished, ask questions about these areas to try and identify precisely what it is they meant to say.**

15. When someone puts forward an argument, identify the key points on which they rely. Make a brief note to remind yourself of these points. Use this to help you to respond.

16. **Consider how you can connect your own ideas to the ideas of whoever is speaking. This will show how carefully you have been listening and will also help the discussion to develop.**

17. Listen patiently, even if you are desperate to speak. Discussion and debate works on the principle of building knowledge together. You are not participating fully if you are only focussed on what you want to say.

18. **When working in pairs or small groups, positively reinforce what other people say. Use phrases such as: 'I see,' 'That is an interesting point,' and so on.**

19. When making notes while listening, try to keep them brief. Listening actively to what is being said is of greatest importance. Notes can always be made afterwards.

20. **Show you have listened carefully by rephrasing what has already been said. This could be as a lead-in to your own ideas or as a clarification of what the speaker meant.**

Language and Vocabulary

1. Use technical vocabulary. This demonstrates your understanding of the subject. An easy way to do it is to identify important keywords before you start. You can then look for places to use them in your work.

2. **Consider your choice of words more carefully. Use a dictionary or a thesaurus to ensure you are picking the correct words to explain what it is that you are thinking.**

3. Practise using the keywords from the topic. Aim to use at least one keyword in each of your answers.

4. **Research three new words which would be suitable to use when writing about our subject. Aim to use these words in your next piece of work.**

5. Replace any slang words you are tempted to use with more formal alternatives. For example: instead of 'my crew' write 'my group of friends'.

6. **When you have finished your next piece of written work, read it aloud. Change anything which does not make sense or which could be explained more clearly.**

7. Create a glossary of all the key terms from our topic. Use this when you do your next piece of writing to ensure you are using the words correctly.

8. **Ensure you choose the right style for the type of work we are doing. For example, a letter needs to be written formally; a story can include jokes or humour.**

9. Always write in paragraphs. Use this rule to help you: One Key Idea Per Paragraph (new idea = new paragraph).

10. **Use PEE for every paragraph you write. P = Point; E = Explain; E = Evidence. This will make your writing clearer.**

11. When doing longer pieces of work, create a short plan. You can use this as a guide. It will stop you straying off topic when you are writing.

12. **When you have finished a piece of work, re-read it and remove any unnecessary words.**

13. When you have finished a piece of work, read it through and then rewrite it. You should aim to say the same things, but with greater clarity and precision.

14. **Ensure each sentence you write follows logically from the sentence before. This will make your meaning clearer for the reader.**

15. Find examples (from textbooks, journals, newspapers and so on) where the technical vocabulary of our subject is used correctly. Copy these examples into your own work.

16. **When you have finished your work, ask a partner to read it aloud to you. Make notes on how you can improve your writing and then make the improvements.**

17. Be sure to include the question in your answer; otherwise it will not be clear to the reader what you are writing about. For example: Q. What is the chance of rain? A. The chance of rain is...

18. **Be consistent in your writing choices. For example, if you begin in the past tense, remain in the past tense. Or, if you begin in the third person, remain in the third person.**

19. Before you begin a paragraph, think through what you want to say. This will help keep your writing precise and to the point. (Avoid beginning to write and then thinking about what you are trying to say).

20. **Think about the demands of the subject. For example, science requires clear, straightforward explanation. Citizenship, on the other hand, expects persuasive argument.**

Developing Creativity

1. In your work, try to develop connections with other subjects. Look for opportunities to make links. This will demonstrate your understanding of how the curriculum is interconnected.

2. **Before you answer a question or complete a task, consider the different options available to you. Identify which is most suited to what you are trying to achieve and then follow it through.**

3. When you have completed your work, look back over it in search of connections you could make. Rewrite some of your answers so that they include these new connections.

4. **Choose an idea we study which you find interesting and explore it in your work. Look at it from different angles; try connecting it to different things; test out its use and its relevance.**

5. Develop your answers by pursuing your ideas as far as they can go. Explore the implications of your thoughts through different scales: small, medium, big; local, national, global.

6. **Combine the ideas we look at with your existing knowledge. By linking concepts together you can discover new ways of thinking about them.**

7. When answering a question or completing a task, consider the alternative options you could use. This could mean the alternatives available before you start, or those which become apparent part way through your work.

8. **Vary your work by using alternative methods of answering questions or completing tasks. For example, supplement your written responses with pictures or diagrams.**

9. When thinking about how to answer a question or how to complete a task, identify a nugget of an idea which you think has the potential to be interesting. Once you have found your 'nugget', work on developing it and exploring it in your work.

10. **Try to pick out the central ideas in a question or a task. Once you have these, consider how you can develop them creatively in your work. This could be through making connections, through trying out different possibilities or through following the ideas in certain directions.**

11. What is your style? Before you begin a piece of work, think about how you will make it your own. Style does not mean going over the top. It means finding a way of going about things which combines your personality with your technical skills.

12. **Try answering questions in a variety of styles. Consider what style might be most appropriate given the nature of the task.**

13. Take risks in your work. This can include: trying new approaches; focussing on specific areas of interest; making connections beyond the subject.

14. **Take risks by trying to push your ideas further. For example, if you are analysing an idea, take that analysis further by extending it to related concepts and real-life situations.**

15. Make comparisons in your work between the ideas and information we look at and other things you know about. Use these comparisons to think creatively about the ideas and information.

16. **Compare what we study with what you know about the world already. Search for similarities and connections and try to weave these into your answers.**

17. Aim to be independent in class. Take decisions on your work and follow them through. This will help you to create responses which are your own, rather than ones which follow a pre-set pattern.

18. **Aim to be original when responding to tasks or answering questions. Consider how you could give an answer or response personal to you and your way of thinking.**

19. Use different viewpoints as a way to think creatively about the ideas and information we study.

20. **Try to develop your answers in new and original directions. Consider how you might take the ideas and information we look at and put you own 'spin' on them.**

Skills of Analysis

1. Explain your answers in more detail. Demonstrate, using more evidence or reasons, why it is that what you are saying is true.

2. **Give examples to support your points. An example connects an abstract idea to the real world, helping your reader to understand more clearly what it is you are saying.**

3. Before you begin a piece of work, analyse what it is you are being asked to do. Make a list and check it with the teacher if you are unsure. Then, use it to help you complete your work.

4. **Analyse what you are being asked to do by identifying the keywords in a task or question. Having picked these out, make sure you do what it is they are asking.**

5. Separate the different ideas you have in response to a question or a task. Deal with them one-by-one. This will make your work clearer and more coherent.

6. **When you finish your work, compare it with the last thing you did. Identify how your current piece of work is an improvement. If it is not, make it better.**

7. Examine ideas and information more carefully. Use these questions to guide you: What are the key elements? How does it connect to other ideas or information? Why might it be important?

8. **Distinguish between the different points you want to make. Separate them out and deal with each one in turn.**

9. When you finish your work, go through and analyse whether you have met the success criteria or achieved the

learning objective. If not, improve you work. If you have, explain how you have done it.

10. **Compare different ideas in your work. Consider how they are similar or different and what the implications of this might be.**

11. When you are writing about a concept, analyse it in more detail. Explain the different meanings it has, or the different ways it can be used. Give examples to support what you write.

12. **When answering questions, explain each point you make in detail before moving onto the next one. This will help make sure you are analysing things in depth.**

13. When given a task, analyse all the separate things you will need to do in order to be successful. Make a list of these and tick them off as you go along.

14. **Before you begin your work, make a quick plan of what you intend to do. When you finish, compare your plan with what you have done. Identify how closely you followed it and whether you need to do anything else (or whether you need to plan differently next time).**

15. When we study our next topic, try to pick out which ideas and information are most important. This will help you to focus on the central elements of the topic.

16. **Spend more time deciding what particular element of the work you will focus on. This will help direct your efforts toward a single goal, rather than spreading them across a range.**

17. When beginning a task or answering a question, consider the different possibilities available. Compare these to the

success criteria and identify which is the best one to follow.

18. **When you have finished your work, swap it with a partner. Identify something they have done well which you could incorporate in your own work. Go back and improve your work accordingly.**

19. Come up with two or three questions which you can ask yourself after every piece of work. For example: 'How clearly have I communicated what I think?' Use these to keep yourself on track.

20. **When comparing ideas or pieces of information, ensure you always give examples to support your points.**

Chapter Eight – Feedback Continued: Criteria

Let me reiterate what I have been saying, and at times implying, about assessment.

Assessment takes place in reference to some set of criteria.

You cannot make a judgement without criteria.

The process involves deciding what something is akin to. It includes:

- Asking whether the item in question does things which are specified in the criteria.
- Asking whether the item in question bears a resemblance or similarity to things specified in the criteria.

For example:

'Arsenal Football Club produced a good performance at the weekend'.

The phrase 'good performance' makes reference to a set of criteria. These do not have to be specific or codified. The speaker may not even be able to articulate them. But they have to exist otherwise the sentence has no meaning.

In this case, let us imagine that the speaker has been watching football for a number of years. They have in their mind a range of examples of what they deem a 'good performance'. They also have a number of examples of specific elements which might go towards making a performance 'good'.

They will also have some general rules or expectations about 'good performances' that they have extrapolated from individual cases (and collections of individual cases) with which they are familiar.

In addition, it is likely they will have internalised judgements made by others either in their presence (such as down the pub) or that have been conveyed to them (such as through the television).

It is also probable that the speaker has the converse of all this – experiences, examples and so on of bad performances. Through this they are also in a position to judge whether they believe a performance to be good or not.

Imagine that the speaker has taken their child to watch Arsenal for the first time. At the end of the match the child, who has thoroughly enjoyed themselves, declares: 'That was a great match! Arsenal were brilliant.'

On what is this judgement based?

Should we accept the child's judgement without recourse to another authority?

We would perhaps take the judgement as evidence that the child has enjoyed the game. We might feel that the child was articulating their delight and pleasure at the experience, rather than offering a sound judgement.

But what do we mean by 'sound'?

Again, we come to the issue of criteria. To use the word 'sound' is to reference an idea of that which we take 'sound' to be and to use what this comprises as criteria by which to judge the item in question.

Let us draw this back to the classroom. The two hundred strengths and two hundred targets given in the previous chapter all make reference to elements of the criteria which we associate with success in education. Here are three cases to consider:

1. **Good use of examples. You have thought carefully about how best to explain your points. This makes it easier for the reader to understand what you are trying to say.**

Why are the examples good? Because they have been chosen with care in order to accurately explain the points. Why is this good? Because clear explanation benefits the reader by making the meaning of the text easier to understand. Why is this good? Because any piece of writing is an attempt to communicate something which is in your head to someone else through the medium of the written word. Clarity suggests: i) a closer relationship between that which is in the person's head and that which they have written, and ii) even if this is not the case, that a meaning of some sort has been conveyed such that it can be decoded.

2. **Ensure your work progresses logically from start to finish, however long it is. The connections between each part of your work should be clear and coherent.**

Why should this be a target? Because it indicates something which is believed to be necessary in order for a piece of work to be judged as good. Why is logical progression necessary for a piece of work to be judged as good? Because logical progression conveys understanding and creates a sense of coherence. These two things in conjunction increase the clarity of the work and, by extension, the ease with which it can be read and understood. Why should a sense of understanding and a feeling of coherency be deemed important? If it can be sensed that the writer understands that which they are writing about, this gives confidence to the reader and, although this is not for certain, it suggests the writer is able to manipulate the material skilfully (what do we mean by skilfully?). Coherence is valued because it fits with deductive reasoning (if a then b, if b then c, therefore if a then c) which is itself held in high regard because of the fact that the proof of its correctness can be assumed from its constituent parts, and therefore without recourse to external criteria (a-b, b-c, therefore a-c. No more is needed to prove this is the case than that which has been stated).

3. Try to develop your answers in new and original directions. Consider how you might take the ideas and information we look at and put you own 'spin' on them.

Why should this be a target? Because we value originality and independence of mind. This is closely associated with dominant moral values in the West. Also, because to put your own 'spin' on something suggests one understands it sufficiently well to be able to reframe it in accordance with one's own ideas and ways of thinking. Understanding is valued because it is confirmation of learning. Learning is valued because it is the successful transmission of knowledge, or the successful facilitation of knowledge acquisition, such that she who has learnt is in a position qualitatively different from where she was before. The learning is a supplement which allows and gives access to things which previously may not have been reachable.

There are two things to note about these examples. First, we could continue the analysis in each case. The point at which I have stopped them is not the end. In example three, for instance, we could question why it is that the increased capacity to do and think is seen as good. Second, I am not suggesting that you need to be thinking in this level of detail when you are giving your students strengths and targets. I have shown this little bit of analysis here so as to indicate the structure which underpins the strengths and targets in this book and that, I am sure, underpins the kind of strengths and targets you are already setting your students.

For a strength or target to be of use to a student, it must reference some set of criteria linked to the learning. In the case of strengths, they should explain to the student what they have done well and why it is that this is a good thing. In the case of targets, they should explain to students what they can do in order to improve and why this will be an improvement.

By including two hundred strengths and two hundred targets in the book, I have attempted to make life easier for the teacher. This is because:

i.   The strengths and targets are complete and non-subject specific. Teachers can read through their students' work, select appropriate strengths and an appropriate target and then copy these out.

ii. The strengths and targets offer a wide range of examples covering different aspects of learning. Teachers can look at these and adapt them to suit their purposes or use them as a starting point for their own strengths and targets.

iii. They give an insight into some of the criteria which underpin Western education. These can be pulled out by the teacher and used as a basis for creating their own strengths and targets.

I am now going to present a second tool which is designed to save teachers time. It is concerned with making explicit some of that which is referred to above in point (iii) – the general criteria of reference in Western education.

General Criteria of Reference in Western Education

Although the curriculum at Primary and Secondary level is split into separate subjects, there are many criteria by which students are judged which are common to most (and sometimes all) of these different areas. If you can familiarise yourself with these, it will help you to assess students' work more quickly and more effectively. It will also help you to give accurate strengths and appropriate targets.

Here is a list of general criteria that you can use to help you. The list is not exhaustive. All the items on it will probably be familiar to you, though you may not have thought about them in this way before:

- **Accuracy.**

This can be used in a number of contexts. For example:

- Accuracy in the use of words in writing or speech.
- Accuracy in the use of words to communicate what one thinks.
- Accuracy in terms of recall.
- Accuracy in the use of a skill.
- Accuracy in the creation of something.

- **Reasoning.**

Subdivisions include:

- Logically correct reasoning.
- Reasoning which is explained.
- Inductive and deductive reasoning (the first is from experience, the second is from general premises).
- Reasoning in support of an argument.
- Reasoning used in conjunction with evidence and examples.

- **Clarity.**

Subdivisions include:

- Clarity of thought (as evidenced through writing or speaking).

- Clarity of communication (which could be through various media).
- Clarity as a result of something else (such as planning or refining).
- Clarity of an element of communication (such as argument or analysis).
- Clarity of purpose.

- **Communication.**

Subdivisions include:

- Writing. This is a large category which contains all those things which go to make up 'good' writing at various levels and in various contexts.
- Speaking. As above.
- Reading. This category is smaller and is concerned with responses to that which is read. This ranges from knowing what the words mean and how to pronounce them to interpreting and evaluating an entire text in light of theory and experience.
- Listening. This category is also smaller and is concerned with responses to that which is heard. This runs from being able to process what others say right through to being able to evaluate what others say in depth and in detail.

- **Bloom's Taxonomy of Educational Objectives.**

The taxonomy is hierarchical. It runs from low-order to high-order thinking as follows:

- Knowledge. Knowing things; being able to recall and remember things.
- Comprehension. Understanding things; being able to describe what things mean.

- Application. Applying things; being able to use things correctly.
- Analysis. Analysing things; being able to explain how things are, what their structure is and how they function.
- Synthesis. Synthesising things; using that which is known in order to create things which are new.
- Evaluation. Judging things; having a degree of mastery such that one can make judgements about things.

- **Mastery.**

This includes aspects such as the following:

- Mastery of a particular word or idea.
- Mastery of a skill.
- Mastery of a process.
- Mastery of a pre-existing form (such as a style or genre).
- Mastery of a method.

- **Reflection.**

It could be argued that this includes introspection, although some would suggest that ought to be in a category of its own. Reflection includes elements such as:

- Being able to reflect on what one has done.
- Being able to reflect before doing something.
- Being able to use reflection to shape decision-making.
- Being able to reflect critically.
- Being able to using reflection to learn.

- **Thinking Critically.**

Constituents of this include:

- Asking questions of that which one comes across.
- Considering multiple perspectives.

- Inquiring as to why things are as they are.
- Analysing and evaluating.
- Searching for evidence.

- **Being Creative.**

Constituents of this include:

- Thinking creatively.
- Doing things which are original.
- Using what one learns to do or to create new things.
- Combining elements in order to make wholes.
- Establishing and exploring connections.

- **Problem-Solving.**

This includes aspects such as the following:

- Using and understanding trial and error.
- Learning from the attempts one makes.
- Deducing and inferring.
- Hypothesising.
- Developing solutions.

As I say, this list is not exhaustive. Nonetheless, I hope that it will prove of use to you. Each category is applicable to many areas of the curriculum. A number of the categories are applicable to all areas. Each one is general and can be couched in the language of a subject or made specific through reference to whatever content is being studied. For example:

i.   Your diagram of a river delta has been produced in an imaginative way, demonstrating that you are thinking creatively.

ii.   Your analysis of why birds have wings has been presented in an imaginative way, demonstrating that you are thinking creatively.

iii.   Your story is highly original, demonstrating that you are thinking originally.

Before we move on, I will give a short summary of the section:

Identify the criteria of reference (or use the ones I have identified) which run throughout education. Use them to develop strengths and targets for your students. This will save you a lot of time.

Specific Criteria of Reference in Education

As well as general criteria, different areas of the curriculum have specific criteria. We might describe these as the criteria of reference of the subject.

There will be things that subjects share, for example:

- In both History and English one must be able to use sentences and paragraphs correctly in order to clearly communicate one's meaning.

And there will be things that are specific to subjects, for example:

- In English one needs to be able to analyse the meaning of poetry.
- In History one needs to be able to analyse the meaning of sources.

Now, I have chosen these examples deliberately. They show the interplay between general and specific criteria. The process of analysis is the same in both cases. It is the act of breaking an item down in order to see how it functions and what its meaning is. However, the analysis of poetry is not identical to the analysis of sources. The two overlap but they also have elements which remain unique.

As such, it is advisable to spend some time exploring what it is that is referred to by phrases such as: 'She is superb at the subject'; 'This is an example of outstanding work in our subject'; 'He is really thinking like a mathematician now.'

If you can do this, and come up with a list of criteria akin to the general ones I have set out above, there will be two major benefits:

1. Your life will be made easier. You can combine the general criteria with your subject-specific criteria and use both or either to identify strengths and set targets. You will not have to start afresh each time you mark a piece of work. You will have created a thinking tool for yourself. One which you can use again and again; one which will save you a lot of time.

2. Your students will profit enormously. This is for two reasons. First, they will be receiving strengths and targets which are rigorously tied to the determinants of success in your subject – the general and specific criteria of reference. Second, you will be able to share these criteria with your students. This will be similar to how you share success criteria and mark-schemes with them. The difference is that both of those refer to specific tasks, whereas the general and subject-specific criteria are applicable across the board. Sharing these with students will really help them to understand what it is that success means in the subject area that you are teaching.

I do not have the expertise to provide lists of criteria for all the subjects on the curriculum. While I have taught a wide range of subjects at secondary level (History, Sociology, Psychology, Religious Studies, Government and Politics and Geography) my original training was in Citizenship. I will therefore provide a list which is indicative of that subject to act as an exemplar:

Subject-Specific Criteria of Reference for Citizenship

- Expression of one's own opinion orally and in writing.
- Active participation in class.
- Active participation outside of class at local, national or global levels (participation is being used here in the political sense of the word).
- Construction of arguments concerning political and philosophical concepts.
- Forging of connections between concepts, ideas and contemporary examples.
- Contributions to discussions and debates through speaking and active listening.
- Thinking critically about information that is presented to you from a variety of sources.
- Knowledge and understanding of key information and ideas regarding politics, economics, the law and the media in the United Kingdom.
- Knowledge and understanding about global issues and organisations and how these relate to the United Kingdom.
- Knowledge and understanding about campaigning and ways in which one might try to achieve change.
- Use of evidence, examples and reasoning in order to make sound, persuasive arguments.
- Being able to consider a variety of opinions as well as one's own.

There are three things to say about this list.

First, it is not exhaustive. To achieve something definitive would be difficult. This is not least because...

...Second, the list is subjective. Another Citizenship-trained teacher would probably agree with some of things I have put, disagree with others, and point out things which I have missed.

Third, it serves to illustrate the overlap between the general and the specific criteria. In turn, it demonstrates that this is something merely to be aware of rather something to which one should pay great attention.

So, when you are developing your own list of criteria:

- Do not worry about whether it is definitive or not.
- Accept that it will be subjective but that this will be within a framework of expertise which you possess in relation to the subject.
- Make use of the general criteria to construct specific criteria (as overlap is inevitable).

To conclude, having a list of general criteria and a list of subject-specific criteria will:

1. Save you time.
2. Improve the quality and consistency of your formative marking.
3. Help you to give students a clear idea of what constitutes success.

Chapter Nine - Factors Militating Against Assessment for Learning

In these final two chapters, we turn our attention to those things in school which might stop us putting assessment for learning into practice. This chapter outlines a range of factors which militate against the method and the following chapter provides a range of solutions.

1) The student-teacher ratio

In every class the students will outnumber the teacher. Only in a tutorial setting is there the possibility of one teacher and one student. It is for this reason, among others, that teaching is not tutoring and vice versa.

The majority of classes most teachers will teach are likely to contain, roughly, between sixteen and thirty-five students. In smaller schools one might encounter smaller classes; so too in GCSE and A Level teaching of optional subjects; and also in schools were students are set according to ability (the so-called 'bottom' sets can sometimes be made up of only a small number of students). Nonetheless, these cases represent the minority. As such, the student-teacher ratio will generally be weighted heavily in favour of the students.

This means the teacher has to find ways of communicating with all students which remain practicable. It would be impossible to explain each task individually to each student. Instead, a quiet atmosphere is ensured so the teacher (one) can speak to the group (many). With most students working, as a result of the instructions received, the teacher has time in which to focus their attention on those who are most in need of support.

The teacher's relationship with their students is different from a student's relationship to their teacher. Let us imagine a class of thirty-three pupils. The following relationships would exist:

i. 33 individual student-teacher relationships in which the student conceives of themselves in relation to their teacher.

ii. 1 teacher-student relationship in which the teacher conceives of themselves in relation to the class as a whole.

iii. 33 teacher-student relationships in which the teacher conceives of themselves in relation to each individual student.

Some pupils may conceive of themselves in relation to the class as a whole. This is not of great import to us because it does not relate directly to the question of the teacher's pedagogy. For the same reason we are discounting student-student relationships in the classroom.

It is the teacher's job to ensure that all students are learning. They cannot help but prioritise their relationship to the whole class. If they subordinate this to individual relationships then they cannot know that the whole class is learning. They must deal with the whole-class relationship first. Individual relationships can come afterwards. If they do not take this approach then they are not fulfilling their role; they are not ensuring the students in front of them are learning.

It goes without saying that teachers will weave their individual relationships into their whole-class communication. It might, for example, take the form of effusively praising a student who has caused great disruption in the past, so as to keep them onside. However it manifests itself though, the premise remains that the teacher will by necessity have to attend to the whole-class relationship.

The prioritisation of this, brought about by the practical demands of the classroom, can make it difficult for the teacher to spend time thinking about students as individuals. It is perhaps easier in a primary school, where a single teacher is likely to spend most of the week with their class. In a secondary school, however, a subject teacher may see as many as fifteen different classes in a week (and will have their work cut out accordingly).

The tendency to become embroiled in the whole-class nature of teaching leads, in part, to the giving out of grades rather than feedback and the ranking of students by a relative measure of ability (relative to other members of the class). An imaginary teacher can help us understand this situation.

Mr Thompson teaches in a secondary school. He is a geography specialist. The school makes geography compulsory in years 7, 8 and 9. It is optional at GCSE and is consistently popular. Mr Thompson has two year 7 classes who he sees twice a week. He also has a year 8 class and a year 9 class, both of which he also sees twice. He teaches two year 10 classes, each for three periods a week. He also has two year 11 classes, one of which he teaches on his own, the other of which he shares with a colleague. This gives him four lessons of year 11 teaching. He has one year 12 class and one year 13 class. He shares both of these and teaches each one for three lessons. The school has 50 minute lessons, six of which are taught every day. Mr Thompson's timetable looks like this:

- Year 7 – four lessons
- Year 8 – two lessons
- Year 9 – two lessons
- Year 10 – six lessons
- Year 11 – four lessons
- Year 12 – three lessons
- Year 13 – three lessons

In total, he teaches 24 lessons out of a possible 30. He therefore has six free periods a week (for which he is forever grateful!).

Let us say that, on average, Mr Thompson's classes each contain twenty-two students. This accounts for the fewer number of pupils in his sixth-form classes compared to those in his lower-school classes. He teaches ten classes. That means he has 220 students, all of whom he is required to assess at regular points.

It is quite understandable to jump from this to the contention that assessment ought to consist of a grade and perhaps a brief comment. 220 is a lot of students. Ten classes is a lot of classes. Mr Thompson does not have the energy to attend to every one of his students as individuals at all times. It is almost inevitable that he will get caught up in the whole-class relationship and will view his students' books in a similar vein.

This is not to Mr Thompson's discredit. As we have noted, the structure of his job militates against him using assessment for learning when marking his students' work. The key for Mr Thompson is unlocking ways in which he can give quality feedback to such a large number of students. He must restrain his whole-class outlook, keeping it only for certain times. It is much easier to do this if one has the tools by which to use AFL effectively. These can be found within this book.

1) Student peer-groups

Students will tend to conceive of themselves in relation to their peers. The understanding of oneself in relation to others is common in our society. Many people (most, perhaps) would agree that their self is, at least in part, predicated on identifications with and oppositions to others. For example: Person A may be a member of a cricket club and strongly opposed to nuclear energy. Their sense of self therefore contains an identification with the cricket club (and the other members of the club) and an opposition to those who are in favour of nuclear energy (as well as an identification with those who are against it).

Young people face a transitional period in which they are finding their place in society. This can involve the rejection of some of the norms and values of their family and a greater focus on peer-group relationships. If this is the case, it is likely that peer groups will reinforce their own norms and values, with these being taken on by the members.

There are two ways in which this can militate against assessment for learning. First, if a group of students see learning as something which is negative, they will be less likely to respond to learning-focussed feedback. Further, they may fail to engage with peer- and self-assessment tasks due to these being centred on learning and the opening up of the learning process.

Second, students may see learning as a competitive experience, one in which they rank themselves against their peers. If this is so, it is possible that feedback which does not contain marks or grades will draw frustration and annoyance. Students will expect work to be returned to them with a summative assessment. They will want to know what this is so that they can place themselves in relation to their peers.

2) Student egos

This point connects closely to our previous one. All of us possess egos in the sense that we have personalities and that these, at times, can be concerned with little but ourselves. Students are no different; they all have egos, although the extent and nature of these egos may differ considerably between students.

In the classroom, ego can play a big role. It can come out through the behaviour of students, as well in the behaviour of the teacher. It has great potential for disruption. In any classroom it should be imperative that all students are able to learn for as much of the lesson as possible. If individual egos become heavily involved in what is going on, there is a good chance these they will detract from that imperative. Certain students (or the teacher) may draw the focus onto themselves. This will be in order to satisfy psychological or emotional needs, rather than to further the learning. It is possible to use one's ego, or the ego of a student, to move learning on (for example, through a charismatic introduction to a subject or a Socratic dialogue between the teacher and a student who is particularly forthright) however situations where this possibility arises are infrequent. It is better for everybody if egos are kept out of the classroom.

This applies to successful implementation of assessment for learning as well. Students may see assessment as a means of fulfilling their psychological and emotional needs. They may use summative feedback as a reinforcing tool. This can be true of students who receive grades of any kind. For example, a student who works at an 'A' grade level may use summative feedback as a reinforcement of their success and as a means to generate good feeling about themselves. Equally, a student whose work tends to be at an 'F' grade level may use summative feedback to reinforce their conception that school is not for them and that they are incapable of learning (and so why should they bother?). In the latter case, the reasoning is being used to protect the ego; no one likes to feel they have failed or to find themselves judged unfavourably against those with whom they spend much of their time.

If students identify assessment with the fulfilment of psychological and emotional needs through the receiving of marks or grades then they may respond badly to the instigation of a new regime. Even if the reasons for such a change are outlined, students will still initially search for an answer to the question (which they may not be able to articulate): 'Why can I not get what I was getting before?' Inherent to this are unmet expectations; those which students have become habituated to through prior experience of summative assessment.

3) Students' previous experience

Students have a great deal of previous experience when it comes to assessment. Unless you are teaching the earliest age groups in a primary school, your pupils will have been assessed on a regular basis by all their former (and, if appropriate, current) teachers. Due to the historic hold of summative assessment it is highly probable that a large proportion of this will have been summative. Students will be used to getting grades, marks or levels for the work they produce.

Before we explore the effect of this, let us digress for a moment. Young people have limited experience of life and the world. A major function of education is broadening their horizons through introducing them to information, ideas and concepts which those who have come before them either discovered, wrote about or did. Nonetheless, this still takes place in a single setting – school – which students will attend in one form or another for a lengthy period of time. Their direct experience will thus be heavily bound up with their experience of schooling. Despite learning about new things in a variety of subjects day after day, they will repeat again and again the experience of being in school and all that comes with this. It is not necessarily a bad thing; in fact it may be a very good thing. It does mean, however, that for some (perhaps many) students the arrival of change will be disconcerting. They are used to repetition and they internalise expected ways of doing things.

If we now return to assessment we can see that if students are used to getting grades, marks and levels then the introduction of a new system of assessment will be, for them, a significant change. Unlike us (teachers), students do not have a wide range of experience on which to call. They will be more likely to see what they know as how things are done. They may well make value judgements accordingly, and rest these on inductive reasoning which is severely limited (we have always done it this way so why should we change now? I've been alright doing it that way up until now – why change? This is who we are; this is how we do things here). These are themes which we see in adult life as well. We may act and think in this way ourselves on occasion, perhaps in the form of an intuitive, immediate response to some change (particularly one over which we feel we have no control). The tendency can be pronounced in children though, with this leading to knock-on effects for embedding assessment for learning in your practice.

4) Parental expectations

All parents will have been students. Many of them will have attended school in the same country as which you are teaching. Some of them may have attended the school to which they have sent their children. You may even have taught the parents of students who are in your current classes.

This means that most parents will have formed some notion of what to expect in relation to school. It is highly likely that this will be based primarily on the experiences which they had. These experiences will form the bedrock of their beliefs about what does happen in school and what ought to happen. Even parents who have experience of schools as adults, who have reflected on whether their own experiences are indicative of general experience, and who acknowledge that change takes place, bringing with it new ways of working, will still retain their own experience of education as part of their wider conception of what school is and how things are done there. This is inevitable. The process helped shape their lives. They were a part of it for a long time. It was and remains important.

Parents may hold the belief that summative assessment is and ought to be the norm. They may expect that the school should communicate grades to them. They may expect their children to be able to tell them what marks they have received for the work they have done. If this is the case, it is probable that the parents are interested in their children's progress and want to know how they are doing. It is unlikely that they will be in a position to question the assumptions which underpin the use of summative assessment. Their focus will be on bridging the gap between home and school.

Parental expectations can influence individual children and the whole school. Both of these can have an impact on teachers in the classroom. In the first case, students may either repeat the requests of their parents (Sir, what grade am I? My mum wants to know) or take on their expectations as their own (Miss, I want you to tell me my grade because my dad says I should know what it is). In the second case, if parents are insistent that they are regularly provided with summative assessment information and that this information is also communicated to students, then there is a possibility that the school will succumb to such pressure and act in accordance with those demands.

5) Whole-school policies

Teachers are expected to work in accordance with the policies set out by their school. These might militate against assessment for learning for a number of reasons:

i.   The school requires teachers to regularly share summative assessment data with students. What 'regularly' entails will be important here. Summative data is necessary even within assessment for learning. However, sharing it with students week after week will significantly detract from any targets you set. It will also reinforce the psychological and emotional responses to grades outlined above. If the school interprets 'regularly' as meaning every week, fortnight or half-term, then it may be the case that this method of feedback comes to predominate in the students' mind, casting a shadow across formative feedback.

ii.   The school requires students to know their grades, marks or levels. If this policy is in place then it puts pressure on teachers to keep sharing such information. This is because it is not specified when the students ought to know the information. The assumption, therefore, has to be that they must know it all the time. Teachers will tend to work from this as they will not want to fall foul of the rules under which they are expected to be operating. Better policies would be: 'Students should know their grades at three pre-defined points in the year' and 'Students should know their learning targets, and have these recorded, at all times.'

iii.   The school has no assessment for learning policy. If this is the case, then it suggests the school does not take the practice seriously. It may be that individual teachers (perhaps many of them) use AFL in their classrooms. If, however, there is no policy in place to formalise the school's stance on the matter, then teachers are not receiving support from senior management and there is a lack of clarity over what is understood as best practice. The remedy is not a prescriptive document which sets out in detail what every teacher *must* be doing. Rather, it is a general policy, specific in places, which supports the use of AFL across the school and makes it clear why it is a necessary part of good teaching.

iv.   The school has an assessment for learning policy which lacks clarity. The purpose of policies is to provide a standardised point of reference for individuals within an organisation which can be referred to across time and space in order to ascertain what is deemed as appropriate in given situations in that organisation. It is a way of saying 'this is what we do and this is how we do it'. Policies do not necessarily have to be adhered to by the letter, but they will provide guidance on what is done and how it is done. If a policy lacks clarity then its functionality is impaired. An unclear assessment for learning policy will not give teachers the assistance which it should. Nor will it give the school the direction which it is meant to provide. Their needs to be coherence between what the school wants in terms of assessment, what the teachers want to do in their classrooms in terms of assessment, and what AFL best practice is seen to be.

v. Whatever the policy is, it does not result in teachers using AFL consistently across the school. We are not suggesting here that a policy ought to impose rigid order on what happens in classrooms. It should, however, reflect and reinforce the assessment ethos of the school. If it is not doing that, or if there is a good AFL policy but it is not reflected in the classrooms of the school, then an individual teacher who is using AFL may find their job harder than it ought to be. This is because students will not be receiving the same messages about assessment across the board. It means that the teacher who is using AFL will be more likely to come up against resistance. This is because the experience, for the students, will be contextualised against that of other classrooms where AFL methods are not used. It is better for everybody if there is consistent use of AFL throughout the school.

6) The approach to assessment taken by colleagues

We have alluded to this in the previous point. If colleagues do not use assessment for learning techniques, for whatever reason, then life is made a little harder for the teacher who does. All of us become habituated. The regimented nature of school life strengthens the habits which form. Students who experience different assessment approaches from different teachers are likely, eventually, to associate these with the individual teacher and their lessons. However, if teacher A comes in and starts using AFL techniques when teacher B has never done so, and has worked with the students for some time, it may be a while before the students accept the new approach to assessment.

Of course, it is nonsense to suggest there is a correct way of teaching, one which every teacher should adhere to regardless of the class and the subject. Yet, it is not facile to identify things which have been shown to work and to present these as best practice. In the case of AFL, the onus is still on the teacher to craft their own pedagogy; it is a large toolkit of techniques, methods and activities which all share certain premises. The teacher has to decide how they will make AFL their own.

It is right then, to identify the approach which colleagues take toward assessment as potentially militating against AFL. The professional position of the teacher is not a valid argument for justifying inductive reasoning (I have always done it this way and never had any problems before). It is a valid argument for supporting the teacher's expert role in making reasoned judgements about pedagogy. It is unlikely that arguments could be made against using AFL which trump the arguments in favour of using it.

A more general issue concerning the approach of colleagues is that of the presuppositions they work under regarding their own role and the generic role of 'the teacher'. For some, the teacher is a 'corrector', a person who knows what happens to be the case; someone who tells students if what they say, write and show is right or wrong.

It is quite natural that this model exists. It works from the following premises, among others:

-   Teachers have been through education themselves.
-   Teachers plan what will be studied and know what it is that students are expected to learn.

- A teacher's job is to ensure students know what there is to be known, in order that they too can complete their education.

Most people would agree that all these premises are true. The problem though, is that they do not by necessity lead to the contention that the teacher ought to be a corrector who identifies what is wrong and what is right. A teacher working with the methods and techniques of AFL will see themselves as more of a coach; they are talking to students about what they have done well and explaining how they can improve. Certainly there will be times when they need to identify what is right and what is wrong in student work, but this will not be their overarching aim.

Successful teaching, which surely must constitute successful learning, is more likely to happen when the teacher presupposes that students need to be guided, that they need to be shown how to improve. It is less likely to happen if the teacher presupposes that students must 'get it right' and learn what it is the teacher knows. Elements of the latter are contained in the former, but they are subordinate to the notion of coaching.

To return to our theme, if colleagues do not share the same presuppositions about the teacher's role then this will militate against the use of assessment for learning. It may mean they are less likely to use it themselves and it will provide students with conflicting messages about how learning takes place.

7) The simplicity of grades or numbers

Grades and numbers are simple.

A B C D E F G

1, 2, 3, 4, 5, 6

45%; 55%; 65%; 75%

They communicate information quickly and clearly, leaving little space for misinterpretation. The numbers and grades used to mark school work are widely understood. Parents, employers and university admissions tutors are three examples of groups outside of school who know what the different marks mean and make decisions based around them.

Simple and effective systems carry within them the temptation of trying to extend their use. In the natural and social sciences, for example, simple, effective theories which appear to explain a single aspect of the world can quickly find themselves being extended so as to cover all manner of things well beyond that with which they were first concerned.

Numbers and grades save time. They indicate clearly and concisely where a student is at in comparison to their peers and in comparison to a set of external criteria. This makes it tempting to give students their grades as feedback for the work they have done.

But we must remember, at all times, that a grade or mark does not tell a student anything about what they have done well, why it was good, what they need to do to improve or why they need to do this.

Here, the simplicity of grades and numbers is shown up. They do not carry enough information to be really useful to students. They neither help them to develop their understanding nor do they show them how to improve their learning. At best, a student might be able to infer some points, general or specific, about what caused them to receive a particular mark or grade for the piece of work they have produced. However, no matter the accuracy of these inferences, they will not – will never – be proved or refuted by a grade or a number.

The explanatory power of summative assessment is limited. In some contexts it is highly useful. In others it is a waste of time, pointless even. What must be considered is the purpose of the assessment. If it is to communicate to employers the different academic levels prospective employees attained in a manner which is quick, understandable and known to be standardised across time and place, then grades and marks are perfect. If it is to help a student to learn, they are not particularly helpful.

8) Overarching assessment philosophy

If, in a school, local district or in a country as a whole, the overarching assessment philosophy is not geared towards assessment for learning, then this will militate against the practice. The extent to which it does will depend on many factors, including the degree of freedom afforded to teachers in the classroom.

What may prove to be of greatest importance, is the way in which this philosophy is taken on by students, the way in which it is internalised, and whether or not they come to see it as the norm. If a country, for example, prizes summative assessment and the government of that country uses its administrative structures to prioritise the status of such assessment then this will inevitably affect what students see as valuable.

The message sent out, either implicitly or explicitly, will be that summative assessment, and all which that entails, is deemed as good or, more prosaically, the only thing which will help one to get on in society.

9) Your previous experience

You went to school. You probably continued your education after that as well. It is likely that you will have experienced a great deal of summative assessment. It may well be that for long periods it was the norm. This means that you yourself might get in the way – either consciously or subconsciously – of your own attempts to embed assessment for learning in your teaching. Your previous experience could undermine or frustrate that which you are now trying to achieve.

10) The amount of time available

The amount of time you have available can effect whether or not you are able to make use of assessment for learning. As we noted, summative assessment can be incredibly quick. There is a temptation to use it because it frees up time.

Initially, getting to grips with assessment for learning will increase your workload. This is inevitable. Making changes of any sort takes time; as does learning something new. There may be points where you do not feel that the extra time spent is generating sufficient benefits.

11) The difficulty of changing your own practice

When we find something that works, we tend to stick to it. All of us become habituated – it is natural. School life, with its rigid structure and repetitive nature, is a fertile ground for the forming of habits (and we use this to our advantage when dealing with students). As such, it is easy to become entrenched in certain ways of doing things. This can make change difficult for two reasons.

First, change represents something new and, therefore, unknown. This does not compare favourably to the safe familiarity of that which we already do, wherein we know what to expect and have accumulated experience to act as our proof.

Second, what we do becomes a part of who we are. Changing elements of our practice can feel like changing parts of ourselves. This means it can be disconcerting; it may make us feel ill-at-ease.

Chapter Ten - How to Overcome the Factors Militating Against Assessment for Learning

1) The student-teacher ratio

The tools provided in this book are the best means to overcome the issue of the student-teacher ratio. We will look at different aspects of the problem in turn, providing solutions on each occasion.

i. There are a lot of students. This means there are a lot of books to mark. It would be easier to give grades.

Using the sample strengths and targets and the general criteria of reference provided in this book, in addition to the subject-specific criteria you create, means that giving detailed formative feedback will be much quicker.

Sections of student work can be marked through peer- and self-assessment. You can then focus on marking major pieces of work which encompass the key learning which pupils will have done over the course of a few weeks. This will lead you to mark less frequently but more effectively.

A target sheet in the front of student books allows you and your students to keep track of their targets. Students can indicate where there is evidence that they have met their targets. This saves you time.

ii. There are a lot of students in each class and it is hard to know where they are all at in terms of the learning.

Use the techniques for eliciting information outlined in this book. The whole-class techniques can all be used while you remain at the front of the room. This allows you to ensure everybody is working while you gather information about students' learning.

iii. There are a lot of students and it is hard to give each of them the time I would like.

We have to be realistic here. It is not possible to teach large numbers and to provide individual tutoring to all students. Through assessment for learning you will come close to achieving the same effect. The formative feedback you provide will be personalised. You will be able to elicit information on where all your students are at and to plan and teach accordingly. You will be able to open up the assessment process for all students and you will be able to give some students targeted support.

iv. Student peer-groups

The two issues we identified were a negative attitude towards learning and a desire for summative feedback. Neither one of these is easy to dispel. The solutions I offer are more in terms of mitigation.

v. A negative attitude towards learning.

You should act as a positive counterpoint. Learning should be praised and opportunities taken to confer approval on students and their work wherever possible.

Speak to students whose attitude is negative and encourage them to tell you what has led to them feeling that way.

Use formative feedback. Many students develop a negative attitude because they continually receive low grades. Take a moment to consider how demoralising this must be. Stress to students that they will only receive grades at certain points in the year (I would suggest on three occasions, perhaps four or five for exam classes). The rest of the time they will receive feedback which explains what they have done well and what they can do to improve. It is likely that over a period of time this will have a positive effect.

vi.   Desire for summative feedback.

Be strong! Don't give in. Explain to students that you will be giving strengths and targets and that these will help them to improve. Outline the reasoning behind this. Indicate that there will be points in the year when grades are shared, but that these times will be decided by you and chosen with good reason.

It is likely that students will persist. Reiterate why you are not giving summative feedback. Remember that you are the professional and you know better than they do.

vii.   Student egos

You are using assessment for learning to help your students. That is why you bought this book – to develop your teaching and to improve their learning. You know that assessment for learning helps to raise achievement. You understand the reasons behind this.

Communicate this to your students. It might not convince them. It might not douse the fire of their egos when they cannot get the grades they want, but it will keep things rational and professional.

If we consider that all students once lived in a time (perhaps before arriving at school) when they did not receive grades, and that during this time they got on pretty well, it is easy to see that a negative response to not getting grades is conditioned rather than innate.

Remind students that there will be points in the year when you will share their grades, but that this will not help them to improve. Tell them that the feedback you give them will show them how to get better. And then do this. Again and again. Students will get used to it and the fires lit by their expectations not being met will die down.

viii. Students' previous experience

You cannot do anything about this. It is their experience for now and forever. It is not worth getting into a debate with them about it. If they say: 'But this isn't how so-and-so does it,' 'Well it's not done me any harm up until now,' or something similar, thank them for their comment and let them know that you will be happy to talk to them about it after the lesson. Then, carry on as you intend. It is likely that students will soon get used to your way of doing things.

One word of warning. If you are not consistent with your use of AFL (including the use of formative feedback) then you are not sending the right message to students. Be careful – do not trip yourself up.

ix. Parental expectations

Whenever you get the opportunity to talk to parents about AFL, do so. Tell them how it works and why it works. Explain that it raises achievement and that it helps every child to make progress. Outline the rationale behind it and the evidence on which it is based. Give them examples to show what you mean. Tell them that you are delighted that they are interested in their children's education. Explain they can help by asking their children to talk to them about their strengths and targets. Indicate that grades will be shared at certain times but that for the rest of the year the focus will be on targets. Point out that, if parents know their children's targets then they can actually help them to make progress at home. This is not possible with grades.

x. Whole-school policies

Do your best. Use as many of the ideas in this book as possible. Buy lots of copies of this book for your colleagues. Buy one copy for your headteacher. Write an assessment for learning policy and present it to senior management. Stress to colleagues that a student who knows what their target is (and how to achieve it) is in a better position to make progress than a student who only knows what their level or grade is. Put on AFL training in school. Contact me and invite me in to do training or give a talk. Explain to senior management how AFL has been shown to raise achievement. Point out that this is what everybody wants and so wouldn't it be great to implement it in your school?

xi.   The approach to assessment taken by colleagues

You might just choose to ignore this and to carry on regardless. If instead you decide to see if you can instigate a little change, I would suggest talking in terms of other people's interests (and thank you to Dale Carnegie for such a wonderful idea).

Assessment for learning helps students to improve their work. Once embedded it saves the teacher a great deal of time. The use of formative feedback and the opening up of the assessment process help students to feel more at ease and more motivated. All of this benefits teachers. So, sell AFL to your colleagues by talking in terms of their interests. I am sure that they will want their students to do better, to save time and to have a good atmosphere in their classrooms. Show how AFL can help to achieve all this. Invite them to your classroom to see you and your students at work. Point them in the direction of this book (or, even better, buy them a copy). Share your resources with them. Offer to help them develop some resources. Set up a group in which teachers can talk about their experiences of embedding AFL in their practice.

xii.   The simplicity of grades or numbers

There is no getting away from the simplicity of grades or numbers. Avoid the temptation to extend their use. Remember this at all times: Grades and numbers do not help a student to learn. Strengths and targets do.

xiii.   Overarching assessment philosophy

There is not a great deal one can do about this, so ignore it. Use AFL, tell your students why you are using it and be ready to justify what you are doing if someone asks. After all, you are a professional who is expected to make decisions and you teach in an education system which prizes reason and the use of evidence. You have made a decision based on reason and evidence. What more could anyone ask?

xiv.   Your previous experience

The best way to deal with your previous experience is to be aware of it. Do not assume that because you have decided to use AFL there will be an automatic step-change in your thinking. Be alive to the fact that your previous experience – which might be deeply ingrained – can still influence your decision-making. Watch out for it and, if you spot it rearing its head, be ready to damp it back down with the cool logic that underpins AFL and which proves why it works.

xv.   The amount of time available

Accept that, at first, getting to grips with AFL will take a little bit of time. It will not be a lot – it is, after all, fairly simple – but it will be more than nothing. Bear in mind that once you are over the first hump, you will actually save a considerable amount of time. This is because you will be marking and teaching more effectively. In addition, you and your students will have a far better understanding of where they are at and how they can improve. This means that, in the same amount of time, you and they will be able to achieve more than was previously the case.

xvi.   The difficulty of changing your own practice

Any change takes a bit of effort. Be persistent. Take small steps. Congratulate yourself on the things you do well. Learn from the things that do not go so well. Keep positive. Remember that the benefits of using AFL are significant and that, in a month or two's time, you will look back and wonder how on earth you ever got by without it.

Chapter Eleven – Conclusion

Assessment for learning is simple. It is also effective.

It involves three things:

1) **Eliciting and using information.**

2) **Opening up success criteria.**

3) **Giving formative feedback.**

If you do each of these consistently, you will help your students to make significant progress. In the long-run, you will also save time.

In this book I have presented a wide range of strategies, activities and techniques which can be used across the curriculum and with a variety of different age groups. Try them out. Find which ones work for you and your students. Adapt them if necessary, or invent your own.

Speak to colleagues about assessment for learning. Speak to students about it. And to parents as well.

Reflect on the premises which underpin the method, and note how sensible they are.

Go out and read the research; see for yourself how much evidence there is in support of the method.

For more ideas on how to elicit information and develop learning, read my other books: 'How to use Discussion in the Classroom' and 'How to use Questioning in the Classroom.' (There are others available as well, but I'm sure you'll be able to find them).

And most of all, enjoy yourself. Teaching is great fun when everyone can see that they are learning and making progress. It is usually very rewarding as well. For the teacher and for their students.

Printed in Great Britain
by Amazon